W9-AHK-840

Acknowledgements

Thank you, Lord, for inspiring everyone mentioned below to follow Your voice and impact lives. To Randy Lawrence – without him, Adventure Community Church would not have happened. And without Adventure and Randy's investment in my life, my story would have a far different ending. Thanks Paul, for trailblazing the book process. To Sheryn and the Book Publishers Network team for making it a reality. To my crack editing team – this book would have been less, absent the help and input of my dad, Roger Snyder, as well as Jeff Price, Randy Lawrence, and Mike Ward. Special thanks to Vicki McCown, literally the best professional editor with whom I have ever worked.

Thanks to all the men who responded to God's nudges by calling me, emailing me, encouraging me, or asking me, "So how's it going with the book?" Thanks to John, Craig, Bart, Morgan, and the rest of the Ransomed Heart team for listening and walking with God. Your obedience and the resulting actions have radically changed the course of my heart. Especially Morgan. The power of your words have guided the creation of this book and held me fast to its course through many dark and hard-fought months. Thank you.

Thanks to my family for their support and long suffering through early mornings and late nights during the book-writing process. To my parents, Roger and Linda, for raising me in a safe, wonderful home, for staying together, for staying with me when I strayed, for constantly praying for my reawakening, and most of all, for celebrating, supporting, and encouraging this journey.

To my amazing wife, Heather – thank you for sticking with me during the dark years and for being my partner in this new adventure. I couldn't do it without you. You truly are the most beautiful woman in the world. I cannot wait to grow old together as we travel the path that God sets before us.

This book is dedicated to my sons, Isaac and Judah, and to men everywhere who seek freedom.

BECOMING UNBOUND:

FROM PORNOGRAPHY TO FREEDOM

EZRA SNYDER

 BOOK PUBLISHERS NETWORK

Book Publishers Network
P.O. Box 2256
Bothell • WA • 98041
PH • 425-483-3040
www.bookpublishersnetwork.com

10 9 8 7 6 5 4 3 2 1

Printed in the United States of America

LCCN 2010914923
ISBN10 1-935359-67-3
ISBN13 978-1-935359-67-8

Editor: Vicki McCown
Cover Designer: Laura Zugzda
Typographer: Stephanie Martindale

CONTENTS

Introduction

don't know the real reason you have chosen to read this book. I can guess, of course. Maybe you heard about it from a friend. Or your pastor recommended it to you. Or maybe you are a woman hoping for some insight into your man. In any case, there are a couple things you should know about this book before you begin.

First, you should know that this isn't a book full of tips, tricks, techniques, or formulas about overcoming something. It's not about accountability or some kind of twelve-step program. Answers to the questions you are struggling with are inside. But just reading these words won't bring change. Action will be required on your part. There, I said it. And hopefully you'll find that refreshing. Truthful. This book is a story. My story. And I genuinely believe that reading my story and then taking action in yours will transform your life.

Second, you should know that this book doesn't mince words. The stories are real, as they happened. You should assume that names have been changed. Because real life – our real stories – are usually messy and painful. We have regrets, we wish we could have done things differently. And there are also experiences we'll remember forever that change our life, our direction, our mission. This book has them all.

Lastly, you should know that this book wasn't written in a vacuum. It wasn't written just so I could say "I wrote a book." No, far from it. This book was put together *for you*. Because of you. Because of your story. I don't know you, but I believe that your story and mine are very similar. Circumstances change, but our thirst for life, our desire for authenticity, for genuine relationships, for *real* life remains constant. So, welcome to my story. And may God shine His light brightly on your story as you read what He has done in mine.

Ezra Snyder

PART I

1
EARLY YEARS

I started masturbating when I was about six years old. I remember squirming around for a minute or two in my bed and feeling a little *zing* of sorts. Nothing really happened except my curiosity was slightly satisfied. Asking lots of men when they started masturbating has led me to believe that you started somewhere around that age too. Makes sense, right? It felt pretty good. And it certainly didn't seem wrong at the time. But it wasn't something that I talked to anyone about either. My recollection is that it happened somewhat regularly, but without any rhyme or reason other than curiosity.

Growing up, my home was a safe, Christian home. My parents loved each other dearly and are still together and still very much in love. My boyhood was spent in Northern California in a tiny ex-hippie, but not quite ex-pot-growing, community. Housing was a 400-square-foot cabin that my dad built. We had a woodstove, no electricity, and running water only because the water tank was higher than the sink. I lived an ideal boyhood, where baths took place only on Saturday night. My parents became Christians a few years after I was born in 1974. And kneeling by that woodstove, I clearly remember asking Jesus into my heart as a six-year-old after a classic and particularly fiery Baptist sermon. Within a year, my dad decided to go to seminary and we moved to Los Angeles. Not so ideal, a difficult transition in my life, but that's a different book. Then at thirteen, we moved to Juneau, Alaska, to pastor a small church. A welcome change from smog and traffic.

The first time I saw pornography was shortly after that move – much later in life than most of the men I know. The ninth grade class was completing a community service project cleaning up the side of a road. I will forever remember picking up that black plastic trash bag with the long-deteriorated bottom. Up I lifted and *whump* – out dropped a pile of magazines. I remember feeling as though a spell had been cast over me. I literally could not look away. The sight of that pile still feels as though it is etched on my memory. In that moment, under that spell, a kind of light bulb turned on for me as a hormone-filled fourteen-year-old. Before that moment, masturbation wasn't usually connected to any kind of porn or fantasy. Not anymore. A singular moment and I was hooked on her, pure and simple. And she felt irresistible.

From then on, porn and fantasy and masturbation were inexorably linked. Considering that I was the pastor's son in a small town, porn magazines were fairly difficult for me to get my hands on. Instead, I looked in books, used my imagination, created fantasy, and watched movies. Rated R was just fine by me. One of my few high school friends, Alex, used to spend hours with me at the video store. Small town, small store. And after we'd seen most every VHS they had, half the fun of hanging out seemed to be spending two hours walking around remembering and making fun of the movies on the shelves. For me, it was a chance to look at the cover, a picture of the beautiful actress, and remember a scene – holding the video in my hand and trying to burn it into my memory. I always lobbied Alex for the new release with the best chance of nudity. Not by name of course, but that was the part of the "R" rating I wanted to see.

In 1992, the summer after my graduation from high school, the "X" rating was introduced. I worked at a local hotel as a bellman. In between carrying luggage and doing whatever was needed, I discovered that the in-room movies had a free five-minute preview. I found myself not being able to wait to go on my two breaks each shift. By the time I entered my first semester at college, everything was available. *Playboy* magazines were everywhere, no more stigma, everybody had them and no one cared. Spring semester brought admittance into a fraternity – even less stigma, even more access, more porn, and more masturbation.

From the moment I first saw pornography, an internal war raged. I knew that I had become a Christian when I was six. But I felt like I could not stop looking at porn and masturbating. It seemed like seasons of strength and weakness came and went. One season I could choose not to look even though options were everywhere. The next season I looked every day or several times a day, feeling like I could not satisfy my desire for more. If you had asked me during those bad seasons if I felt addicted to pornography or masturbation, I would have answered emphatically "No." Why emphatically? Because addiction was a word describing alcoholics and drug users, not guys who struggled with porn and masturbation. Sure, I wanted to stop, but I didn't believe I had enough strength to stop. But I knew that I would stop when it really mattered. In fact, since freshmen year in college I had known when I would stop looking at porn and stop masturbating. And when was that supposed to be? When I got married to Heather, whom I had met freshman year in November, 1992. I was absolutely convinced beyond a shadow of doubt that I would stop once I got married.

I had convinced myself that this was true – because surely once I started having sex, porn and masturbation would become less interesting. Part of me didn't even really want to be looking at porn and masturbating. I didn't feel better or stronger afterward; I actually felt weaker. But that part of me got overruled most of the time by the part of me that felt like it was irresistible. That I just couldn't control myself, couldn't help myself. So it seemed natural enough to decide that my craving would be satisfied in marriage. Growing up in the home that I did, I had firmly vowed to myself to wait until marriage to have sex. To this day, I do not really understand how or why I believed that so strongly, but I did. Navigation through this season in my life was a complex imbalance: falling in real love with Heather; trying to stop doing something that I was convinced I couldn't stop doing; and rationalizing that my growing addiction to porn and masturbation was somehow the right thing for both of us.

As I moved through sophomore and junior years of college, the degree of my descent into porn and masturbation did not increase, but the frequency certainly did. I doubt more than a week ever went by without me finding someone else's magazine, staying up late to watch HBO or Cinemax, or renting a movie and watching a particular scene over and over again. It just became a habit. Occasionally it happened at the last minute. Sometimes I looked forward to it all day. Rarely would a day go by without at least thinking about either porn or masturbation. They became at minimum a weekly habit.

Senior year, the degree worsened. During my bachelor party somebody brought a video and put it on. At first I didn't really notice it because I was in another room in the fraternity house playing poker. Toward the end of the party, quite a few guys had gone home. The video was quietly playing in the corner and for the first time, I saw the difference between the X-rated movies I had grown accustomed to from my summer hotel job and real, hardcore, XXX-rated pornography. And just like on that roadside years ago, I was hooked instantly. I remember the next afternoon going to the guy who had brought the movie and asking him if I could borrow it for another bachelor party I was going to that night. A lie, of course. What I did was go home and watch that video half a dozen times over the next couple days. And somehow that was a tipping point. Before that, I had never actually spent any money on hardcore porn. I had always managed to "borrow" a magazine and put it back later or just rent the R-rated movie or watch cable TV. After watching that movie, I began looking for stores that rented movies like that and frequenting them. There was a little bit of stigma remaining, walking into the Adults Only section. Actually, walking out carrying something seemed slightly more scary. But after a few times of seeing the look on the clerk's face and knowing he really didn't care, the stigma vanished. And what remained was just the feeling that I wanted more. Porn felt so irresistible.

All this was going on in the two months before I was to get married in May, 1996. It seems so foolish now, looking back, but even in those two months, I was convinced that I would stop as soon as the real sex started. A little part of me thought that I'd better get all I could while it was still okay, before we said those vows. The wedding day came and went; the honeymoon came and went. My battle with porn and masturbation remained.

I'll share with you in more detail in later chapters how all this affected my wife, our wedding night, and our lives. For now, the important note is that I remember really being surprised. I had convinced myself that it would disappear, that my desire for porn and masturbating would just evaporate the day I got married. Rude awakening – it did not. So I did what most of us do...I moved on to the next false hope! Joking aside, I just convinced myself that the real stopping point would be when we had kids. But that wouldn't happen for another seven years.

2
DARK YEARS

Professional life went well for me immediately after graduation from college in 1996. Sales were up, profits were up. I owned and ran an office selling Cutco Cutlery that was ranked #7 in the US out of more than 400 offices. Heather was also working full-time and we made over $100K the first year out of school. None of that money and none of the accolades seemed to satisfy my growing desire for porn. I found myself still entranced by the sight of it, by the sight of her, whoever she was. Porn felt irresistible. I learned to hide my use, though. My interest wasn't as spontaneous as it had been during college. I began to look forward to an evening by myself or a weekend when Heather went away. I often worked late at the office, which was now equipped with a TV and VCR. Meanwhile, Heather and I were doing well, enjoying each other, enjoying marriage, and enjoying sex. It was a strange dichotomy – I was having lots of good sex with my beautiful, amazing wife, but I still felt the pull of pornography.

The other significant change during this time in my life was how I felt about looking at pornography and masturbating. During college, rationalization was easy. Now married, I found it far more difficult to excuse this behavior. I had the usual married guy's arsenal of "It's that time of the month" or "She seems tired, I'll give her a break" or "Since she's not coming through for me, I'll just take care of myself" and all the like. But deep down, I didn't really believe the rationalization. I felt bad. Although the porn still really felt like it captured me, when I was done masturbating, I never felt great about myself. I felt weak, like a loser, a pervert, dirty, different. Because something else had also changed with getting married.

I always knew at a cerebral level that my looking at porn wasn't good for Heather. But now I could see that with my own eyes. I could see how after masturbating, I looked at her differently. I could feel how my desire for her was stunted or twisted after spending a bunch of time in front of a video. I remember taking care of business at the office and then coming home to a wife who wanted to have sex. I remember the confusion, the questioning look in her eyes, and the pain when my desire was not fully present. I had given it away to the other woman on the screen. Heather knew that from time to time I had a bad day with pornography, but she had no idea the extent of my struggle. In hindsight I can see how much it hurt her. But that realization was visible only in hindsight. In the moment, we were just two newlyweds trying to figure out how marriage and sex were supposed to work.

In 1999, three really significant things happened. One, the film *The Matrix* opened – but that is another book. Two, I was introduced to the Internet. Three, my professional life took a turn for the significant worse. 1997 was the best year my sales office ever turned in. 1998 was mediocre but found me losing heart and questioning whether or not selling Cutco was the right job for me. In the midst of that, or maybe because of it, I had the two worst quarters ever, lost $65,000, and declared bankruptcy in July 1999. Failure at a professional level brings a lot of baggage with it at the personal level. I took my failure and tried to drown it with porn and masturbation. When I was with those two companions, I did not feel quite so worthless or unhappy, at least for a brief moment.

I was literally at the video store almost every day during those years. Renting hardcore movies, leaving the office early, and going home to masturbate. Silently hoping Heather would some-how find the movies I had carefully hidden so I wouldn't feel so alone. Praying that God would somehow magically just take this away from me so I wouldn't have to bear it anymore. In the end, even after short periods of freedom — a week, ten days, maybe a three-week stretch here and there — I always seemed to find my way back to porn and masturbation. Back to the place I thought would provide comfort, to my feeling taken care of, feeling more like a man.

The next few years are difficult to talk about. Professionally, I tried out insurance for a while and then began working for a small start-up software company. Got transferred to North Carolina and then laid off before 9/11. Moved back to the Northwest and started a series of jobs working for small start-up companies in the middle of the tech bubble aftermath. Layoff after layoff. Failure after fail-ure. During this period from 1999 to 2003, my life with Heather was also extremely difficult. The stress of bankruptcy, of packing up and moving across the country away from all her family, of her carrying a big part of the financial burden when I was laid off. And through all those times, when things got rough or I wanted comfort, I inevitably turned to porn and masturbation.

2001 and 2002 saw the switch for me from hardcore movies to the Internet. Free. Always available. Safe. Nothing to hide except some browsing history and maybe a few carefully stored downloads for later. The same cycle over and over again. Seasons of freedom, of deleting everything from my computer, of feeling more free, but always falling back to the old friends of porn and masturbation. I did hold onto some level of hope during this period that I would finally have the strength to stop once my first child was born. Especially if it was a son. I so wanted him not to have this same struggle. I so wanted him to experience freedom and purity. And yet I literally felt like I couldn't help myself. A part of my heart did not want to look, but the siren song of porn seemed irresistible. And once she was up on the screen, masturbation always seemed to follow.

The hope of freedom seemed to always fall victim to another core belief, one we haven't talked about yet, the underlying identity I came to believe about myself over this decade-long span of porn and masturbation: *I would always struggle*. That somehow, this was just my struggle, the thorn in my flesh that God was constantly challenging me with to see how strong I was. And since I almost always lost, the truth had to be that I was just a weak man and would always struggle, that I was somehow dirty or different. And I believed it.

3

BOTTOM OF THE BARREL

The summer of 2003 I found myself laid off for the fifth time in five years. Professionally, I was dying. I hated my usual sales/marketing gig in the tech industry, doing the same things I'd been doing for the last five jobs. After losing a twelve-week-old in-utero child in early 2002, Heather became pregnant later that year and Isaac was born on May 19, 2003. We found a local church that didn't seem to be entirely full of crap. We got involved. I was in the worship band and on the leadership team for the church. I felt like such a fake. Trying to look like a Christian. Terrified that one day it was all going to come out and I would be found out, exposed. Deep down, some part of me knew I was dying. I knew that something had to change soon or I was going to implode.

I'll never forget the lowest moment of that summer. I was sitting on my back porch with my friend, Andy. He and Lisa had befriended Heather and me. In looking back, they were some of our first real friends ever. He was the worship pastor of the small church that we attended. We had become friends, worship band-mates, and business partners in a small window cleaning company. One evening we were talking about another member of the church, Jeff. He had recently told his wife that he was leaving her and his two sons aged three and five. It came out that he had a huge porn addiction, had found someone online, gone out of state for a job interview, and consummated the affair. Andy and I were talking about how the holes we dig for ourselves just get deeper and deeper and deeper. He made the observation that "You never know what's really going on with people..." and something inside of me cried out. I desperately wanted to cry out to him, to tell him how I had been struggling for so long, how I didn't want to look at porn but felt like I didn't have a choice. But I didn't tell him. I couldn't admit that to my best friend in the world. What would he have thought of me? That I was weak, that I was different, a pervert, an undisciplined man. So I did what most men do in that kind of scenario. I lied right to his face. I got on high moral ground and talked about how porn leads to affairs and how you shouldn't look at it and how sad for Jeff and his family and all other sorts of self-righteous crap.

In the long, nearly sleepless night that followed, I remember trying to make sense of this place in which I found myself living. I knew I was a Christian. I knew that I had really accepted Christ in my heart kneeling by the woodstove in 1980. But deep down, I really didn't get it. People talked about how God changed their lives or what they had heard from Him or how He was using them to do great things or blah blah blah. Honestly, I just tuned them out. For me, my relationship with God looked like this: One, I knew He existed. Two, I knew that I was a Christian, so hell was taken care of. But heaven, honestly? I remember hearing someone say once that they couldn't wait to get to heaven. And I was like...really? I mean, seriously? You can't wait to go someplace where the chief activity is singing hymns for 10,000 years? As I heard someone else say once: "That sounds a lot more like hell to me!"

But that was really the state of my relationship (or lack of relationship) with God. If I got a job offer, then God must have wanted me to get the job. The Bible was a history book, full of rules and the occasional interesting story, but without any real relevance or impact on my life. The Holy Spirit? What could He possibly have to say to me? God? He had told my dad to go to seminary, given him a church in Juneau, Alaska, and then allowed him to get chewed up and spit out by a that church. What good could He possibly have in store for me? Not much, my life experience had told me. If I was living the true offer of Christianity, then I was pretty sure I didn't want anything more to do with God.

The next eighteen months were spent treading the murky sludge left at the bottom of the barrel. New baby, new job, involvement at church. All the while living a series of lies. On the outside, my life probably appeared like it was going fine. I put my business-man hat on when needed, and the window cleaning business started doing well. I put my worship band drummer hat on when needed, and the music sounded good. I put my new dad hat on when needed, and family life seemed okay. Through it all, though, I never stopped believing that I was always going to struggle with porn and masturbation. They were both always there whenever I needed them – ready and waiting to provide solace and comfort.

Fall 2004 brought several significant life transitions. My wife and I became pregnant with our second child. Added busyness, added financial stress. The small church we had been attending closed its doors. That was hard, but Heather and I losing our two sets of really good friends (the pastor and worship pastor families both moved away) was incredibly painful. Then a new church opened in Duvall, Washington, on October 17th, the same day our old church closed. We couldn't actually bring ourselves to attend the new church right away. But after we mourned the loss of Cedar Ridge Church in our lives, we started attending Adventure Community Church.

A few weeks later, I found myself sitting at a table with seven other guys for a men's event at Adventure. It was a Wednesday night in January 2005. I knew one of the guys from Cedar Ridge. We were talking about our lives at a depth that I was not used to. Talking about things that went wrong in our lives. Regrets we had. Decisions we would have liked to make differently. Events that we wish would never have happened to us. My church experience up to this point had not prepared me for this. I was used to being preached at. Told what's right and wrong. And when someone opened up and said, "I struggle with this or that" or "I need help with my marriage" or brought up any other real-life problem, the response was to tell him what to do. We've all experienced this, right? The guy gets up the guts to say he struggles with alcohol and the response is some form of "just stop" along with some kind of spiritual platitude about his body being a temple.

But this night, at this table, guys were actually talking about real life. About struggles with their wives, with their marriages, with jobs, with life. And we were all listening. No one preached or quoted Scripture or called people a sinner. How crazy! But something in me was hooked. It felt real. What church should be like. So I asked the pastor, Randy, if we could spend some one-on-one time together to talk. And he said yes.

Randy and I started meeting, no real structure, just talking about life. And I was amazed at what I was willing to share with him. Somehow I trusted that he wasn't going to lecture me about what

I needed to do or change. So I really opened up. We talked about my life as a child and adolescent, growing up while my dad went to seminary. We talked about being a pastor's kid. We talked about marriage and being a dad. We talked about how my experiences had brought me to certain conclusions about life, about God, and about myself. And we talked about porn and masturbation.

I will never ever forget that conversation. I had a long answer to the question he asked me. I don't recall the question exactly, but I'm sure it was something along the lines of "So how is it going for you with porn?" But I do remember my answer. I remember so wanting to give a good answer, an answer that Randy would like. One good enough so that even after hearing it he would want to still meet with me. So my answer was full of rationalizations, excuses, all the reasons why porn had become irresistible to me, why I couldn't stop and every other justification I could think of. I thought I wrapped it up pretty well, honestly. I concluded by saying, "So I guess I'm just one of those guys who will always struggle with this." Randy paused for about three seconds, looked me right in the eye, and said, "Dude, that is total bullshit."

Now, you have to understand what was going through my mind in that moment. My pastor's kid radar was flashing red because *pastors aren't allowed to use that word!* At the same time, my heart leapt at the idea. Really? Truly? I could be free? But way deep down, another voice came out – one of anger. How dare Randy talk to me about that! How dare he suggest this thing that has ruled my life for well over a decade might not rule anymore? Or that I even have a choice in the matter? What did he know? Looking back, I think my heart was split. A kind of no-man's land between hoping I could have freedom in this area and fearing I never could. I couldn't believe either option fully because I found a bit of refuge in both. It seemed like it was going to take a long time to get used to the idea that something I had found so irresistible for so long might not be.

4
THE ISLAND

There were several things at Adventure that I wasn't used to experiencing at church. Certainly one was having real conversations about real issues as men. Another was hearing from God. This one took a while to sink in. I grew up a pastor's kid, but I never heard of this idea in church before Adventure. My perception of a relationship with God did not involve communication – real, two-way communication, at least. I had learned that God speaks to us through the Bible. But as I mentioned before, I was at a place in my life where I didn't think the Bible had any real relevance to my life, so how could I possibly hear God through that? Then there was the ever popular "open door/close door" concept of communication with God. That had always seemed a bit ridiculous to me. I mean, you pray for God to open a door, you get a job offer, that must be God opening the door, right? So closing the door looks like not getting the offer – great, very helpful to my life. I think I perceived God as a nice guy who played His role a bit like the chess master in the sky, moving pieces around here on earth. But how important is a pawn? I mean, that's all a guy consumed with porn and masturbation could be, right?

While I tried to figure out what I thought about this whole hearing from God thing, I noticed something different about many men at Adventure. Most of my life, I saw men in church as just like me. We had grown up in the church focusing on sin management, where the ultimate goal was to sin less rather than live more. Performing one's duty, being a good husband, serving the church, maybe even one day becoming a deacon, etc., etc., etc., blah, blah, blah. That never appealed to me. But these guys were different. They had friends, not just acquaintances. My whole life, I've wanted a best friend. Someone who really knew me and still liked me. Who thought the same way I did. I never really had one. In fact, I felt like I really didn't have one true friend. Sure, my wife and I invited lots of people over for dinner and had a good time, but acquaintances aren't true friends. That slowly started to change for me because of the investment of the pastor, Randy, in my life.

One of the most powerful moments of my life, experiencing God's heart toward me through another person's actions, happened one afternoon with Randy in the spring of 2005. The prior week I had shared some very difficult parts of my past with him. Painful memories of things that had happened to me during seventh grade. Going from being great at sports to terrible in one pubescent summer. Suddenly I could not hit a baseball. At all. And the self-loathing that comes after a failure like that. The shame. Walking back from the plate to the dugout, shouting in your own mind, "Don't cry, don't cry, don't cry" because you are so ashamed of yourself and your performance. I had shared all this with Randy the week before, including the fact that after seventh grade baseball, I vowed not to play organized sports again. Church softball? Forget about it. Absolutely terrifying to me, and I had no interest in embarrassing myself all over again. A pick-up football game? I'd play only on defense, because I certainly couldn't catch the ball.

So I showed up at Randy's office the following week, he stood up, grabbed two mitts and a baseball off his desk, tossed me a glove and said, "Let's play catch." *Pause.* I'm not sure what to type right now. Or what words would accurately convey the depth of love and care that simple action communicated to me. Not only had he listened, but he actually heard my heart. And he had taken action and found a way to love me precisely where I was at. I will long treasure those few minutes of playing catch outside the church office – everything it silently told me about my value, my worth as a person, of the care and love another human being could show me. Although if I'm honest with you, I did worry a bit about my performance, about whether or not I would catch each ball. Mostly because it was hard to see through my tear-filled eyes.

That afternoon was maybe the first time I can remember in my life understanding anything at all about how God feels about me. I mean, if this random pastor guy who (from my perspective) didn't even really know me would take the time to do something like that for me...wouldn't God do the same or more? In hindsight, that afternoon helped move some of my head knowledge about God – yes, He loved me, the Bible told me so – and made it real in my heart. And that prompted me for the first time to want more. Looking around at these guys whose lives seemed more full, more alive than mine, I started asking them how it happened. Their answer? To a man, the same: Hearing from God is what changed their life. Experiencing God in a personal, real, intimate conversation transformed their life, their heart, their identity forever.

This is not a book about hearing from God. There are books out there on that topic. I will personally recommend a couple in later chapters. But, considering how crucial the concept of hearing from God is to this story and to my journey to freedom, it is imperative that you know where I came from on this topic. I had never heard of hearing from God before. The concept was brand new. But I saw its effect on men whom I respected, and I wanted that experience. I wanted it badly. I didn't know what to do, didn't know the direction, the course, the way – in any sense of those words. I knew only that I wanted something more from life. From church. From God. I wanted more for the first time I could ever remember. Desire to hear from God became the goal of my life in the following season.

Later that spring, I received an invitation. Show up on Tuesday night at Adventure to find out a little bit more about what the next step in your journey might be. Five leaders, seven new guys including me. That night I learned the invitation offered more. More fellowship, a couple retreats during the summer, a trip to Colorado, more time with God, more about my story and my journey. It took about thirty seconds to decide I was in.

What an introduction to a church mentor program! There were about fifteen or sixteen of us meeting at a guy's house over the weekend. Sharing life, sharing struggles, having a real conversation as men. The focus of the retreat was hearing God's voice. How it works. I remember being stunned at the sheer number of examples of this happening in the Bible. How did I miss them all? When had I decided that those were all exceptions instead of examples? I found myself rapidly dismantling all my objections. I simply wanted to experience God *more* than I wanted to have a theological argument over whether or not I could. During several of the times dedicated to pursuing God, to inquiring of Him, I simply sat in a chair and prayed. It took some getting used to. I hadn't prayed and actually wanted to hear a response – ever. Prayer had always just been the help desk, the queue to get in if you wanted to order something better for your life. So it took some getting used to, this idea of sharing with God how I was really doing. Sharing with Him what I really wanted. At that first retreat, I did a lot of listening but almost no hearing. There was too much noise in my head, too many thoughts. And I couldn't help remembering that I had looked at porn and masturbated the night before.

A huge debate was taking shape in my mind. Can a guy who does that kind of stuff hear from God? Is God interested in talking to that guy? I didn't know the answer. When we came together and talked as a large group after those times I spent alone, what the other guys shared ran the gamut. Several men shared what sounded embarrassingly like Psalms. Long verses of platitudes about how good God was and how wonderful He is and how He changes lives and on and on. I found it uncomfortable to listen to. I couldn't tell if that was them actually hearing from God or just reading aloud things they had thought up and written down. Then my future friend Chris shared about his struggles with pot. I was blown away. I mean, we're at a church mentor retreat. And he is seriously talking about struggling with drinking too much beer and smoking pot. It was crazy. I kept waiting for one of the pastors to interrupt him. But no one did. I remember sitting in that circle of guys, mouth shut, absolutely shocked. It wasn't like the other guys heard him and didn't care; they did hear him and I believe they did care. But they seemed to care more about hearing his heart than about telling him how to fix whatever it was he presented as a problem in his life.

That moment, sitting in that circle, was the first time in my life I remember thinking that someday I might be able to talk to others (besides Randy) about my own struggles with porn and masturbation. A couple months later I had the chance.

I showed up a little after 7 a.m. on a Friday morning at Adventure for the next mentor retreat. I wore camo and hiking boots because the word was that we were going to be doing some intense physical activity involving lots of dirt, mud, and possibly submersion in water. My father, who had left the church in Juneau and recently moved to the area, had decided to join me on the retreat. He and I waited with eleven other guys, not knowing what to expect. Soon we were greeted by five leaders who shivered visibly in the chilly morning air, each one's pants already soaked through.

To prepare us for the day, they said we were going to watch a short film clip. Up on screen the beach landing scene from *Saving Private Ryan* flashed. You've seen it, right? The boats unloading on the beach in Normandy. Machine guns, death. Afterward, we debriefed the clip.

"What was going on for you?" they asked. "Fear? Excitement?"

I spoke up and said I was feeling torn between two characters in the clip – the one guy who gets his head blown off the minute the gate drops and the other who is throwing up the entire boat ride in.

The day was spent in a great paintball war. Anointed captain of the invading team, I was given a sweet paintball weapon and an outdated aerial view of an island in the middle of a river that I was supposed to lead an assault against. I was terrified. Of failure, of making the wrong decisions, of leading my team to defeat instead of victory, of what they might think of me if that happened. To say that the assault ended in a draw doesn't quite capture how memorable it was.

So with that backdrop, we began a retreat where the entire goal was to continue learning to hear God's voice. I clearly remember Saturday morning, the first time alone we had. I found a quiet spot along a small branch of the river across from the main camp and sat in the shade for an hour. I really wanted to hear from God. I wanted to hear His voice in the quiet places of my heart. I prayed fervently and with as much desire as I ever have in my life. Then I had a disturbing realization. It was as if God showed up with His palm facing toward me in the "stop" position. And I felt like He was saying He wanted to talk with me, but I needed to deal with what was getting in the way. The obstacle of porn and masturbation. In that moment, I knew I had to get right with God, get this thing I had hidden for so long out in the open before I could experience an intimate relationship with Him.

Later that afternoon we had another designated time with God. A long walk around the island netted an even stronger sense that I had to deal with this issue before I could continue on in my journey. After dinner that night, there was a time of sharing in a large group. Nineteen guys sitting around a campfire on an island in the middle of a river, talking life. But unlike previous sharing times, this one didn't seem to be going deep. A few guys talked about this or that. To be perfectly honest, I don't really remember what was said during the first hour. I was as scared as I have ever been in my entire life. I knew, absolutely knew, that I had to get my struggles off my chest. I knew that I had to tell the group about the terrible burden I had been carrying for so long. But I was terrified. Of what they would say. Of what they would think of me. Of being expelled from the mentor group after I told them the awful truth about who I really was. Of disappointing my father. And terrified of letting my secret out, because once it was out what would happen to it? Honestly, there was a lot of fear tied to letting it out because I had come to rely on porn and masturbation to feel good, feel comforted, feel at least a little like a man for a short time whenever life got too tough. In the deepest place in my heart, though, I had finally arrived at something I wanted more than porn or masturbation. What I wanted was to not be *that guy* (the guy who will always struggle with porn and masturbation) any longer.

So I sat in the circle, quiet. At each pause, I was alternately ready to leap up and start talking or run for the hills. I just could not find the strength to say anything. Finally, seeing the discussion was not going anywhere deep, Randy turned to Tom, one of the other leaders, and said something along the lines of "Let's move on to your part of the talk."

I remember with perfect clarity interrupting Tom.

"I need to share something," I said. "Please don't move on until I can."

In the moments of silence that followed, part of my brain was screaming, "Don't do it! Just figure out a good lie. Don't go there!" while the rest of me really wanted to tell these men the truth. And finally, after years of hiding and feeling alone and ashamed, I did. Clearing my throat for the forty-seventh time that night, I said, with tears in my eyes, "I've struggled with porn and masturbation for the last fifteen years."

I shared a bit more with the guys. That I didn't want to struggle anymore. That I felt like I had to get this out in the open, that I wanted more from God and talking about my struggle was the start. I shared that I did not know what to do or where to go next. I don't know what I expected to happen when I finished talking. But something totally crazy, something completely unexpected happened. It blew my mind. After a few moments of silence, a guy across the circle from me said, "Me too." And then another guy said, "Me too." And another. And another. And another. Guy after guy after guy that night, coming clean about their addictions to porn and masturbation. How they, too, were convinced they were the only one struggling. And what united us all? The desire not to be *that guy* anymore.

The date was July 22, 2005, the day I now refer to as my own personal D-Day. My own personal day of declaring freedom from porn and masturbation. The day I started to believe maybe I didn't have to be *that guy* anymore.

That night we had an epic bonfire. Something deep in my soul was burned out. Cleansed, maybe. I don't know the right word. One of the men offered to baptize me in the river. An offer of renewal and cleansing. I woke up Sunday morning and was baptized along with several other guys. My father, who had also shared his own journey with porn and masturbation the night before, prayed over me – a prayer of thanks, of hope, of friendship, and of freedom. As he prayed, something was left behind on that sand bar in the middle of the Skykomish River. For the first time in my life, I not only felt like I didn't have to be *that guy* anymore, but I also felt like maybe I wasn't.

5

THE JOURNEY BEGINS

eturning from that mountaintop experience into the real world was a challenge. I remember arriving home, unloading the backpack, glancing over at the computer, full of garbage, calling to me. Even though I didn't want to be *that guy* anymore, that didn't mean the temptation was gone. And wouldn't you know it, the very next Friday, just five days after I had declared my freedom from porn and masturbation, my wife and infant went away for the weekend. I was terrified of what I was going to do, of what was going to happen. For the past twelve years, coming home from work on Friday night to an empty house meant a major porn binge – downloading all night, curtains closed all weekend.

I can see myself like a movie clip in my mind, that Friday night, about 7:30pm or so. The comedy I had rented had ended, and I was sitting in my office chair, looking at the computer screen. And the craziest thing happened. My fingers started typing on their own. Muscle memory or subconscious desire, I do not know. But suddenly I was staring at the URL on the screen, my pinky poised over the "Enter" button on the keyboard. In that moment, I remember all sorts of thoughts coming to mind. All the old ones, of course. *Why not? It's not like you'll ever really be free. If you don't fail now, you'll fail for sure later, so why punish yourself by waiting? What's the hold up? You already know you are going to look.* And my personal favorite – *you know you're a different guy, but you haven't really said goodbye to this stuff. How about just one more glance for old times' sake.* Crazy stuff, but I know that you've heard those same messages as you sit in your chair.

Somehow, I'm not exactly sure quite how, I picked up the phone and called my friend Adrian, one of the leaders who had been on the island.

"Dude, I'm sitting in front of the computer, and I'm worried that I'm going to blow it."

Great conversation opener. Three hours later, I hung up the phone. The only thing on the computer I had touched since picking up the phone was the off switch on the power strip. And that one small action felt great. I felt fantastic, strong, like I could conquer the world in that moment of choosing strength, of choosing freedom. I wish I could tell you that from then on everything was easier and I was never in that situation again, but I can't. It doesn't work like that. The journey does get easier, but over time, decision by decision, choice by choice. So what did the following night look like? I spent another three hours talking to Adrian! Because that is what my heart needed in that moment. Victory looked like a phone call to a friend.

The next few weeks were a blur. All sorts of questions crowded into my mind, like "What did the island really mean?" and "Is this freedom real?" and "Will it last?" and "Am I strong enough to win this battle?" But a deep desire to hear from God took the forefront. Was He happy with my island decision? What did He think about it? Would He talk to me now that this huge, blocking sin issue was out of the way? Those were the questions I shared out loud with nineteen other guys, most of whom had been on the island with me. We were preparing to go on another retreat, this time to Colorado for four days. We met four times before our trip to pray together, sharing our fears, our hopes, and our dreams of what the retreat would look like for each of us.

Landing in Colorado I felt equal parts fear and excitement. Would God really speak to me? (Excitement) What would He say? (Fear) The first evening session was all about the heart of a man – how we were designed by God to be strong. I woke up on Friday very hopeful of some time to pursue God individually during the day... to really pursue His heart, to inquire of Him about me. There were three worship songs that morning. I can recall only one of them – "Famous One" by Chris Tomlin – one of my favorite songs to play the drums to, just a joyful and celebratory song. As I was singing at the top of my lungs, I felt a rush of emotion unlike any I had ever remembered experiencing before. I couldn't stand upright. I sank to my knees, overwhelmed at something I did not understand. On my knees, overcome with emotion, tears flooding my eyes, I heard God say the most powerful three words ever: "I love you." For the first time in my life, I knew what it was like to hear God speak to my heart. To experience the still, small voice booming with more power, more truth, more rightness than any I've ever heard audibly in my entire life. He told me exactly what I needed to hear. He told me the thing I couldn't have believed before the island – that He loved me. For the first time in my life, I began to believe God loved me. Not because my head told me so, but because my heart knew it was true. And transformation began.

6

BECOMING UNBOUND

Fall 2005 was an exciting time. I became more involved at Adventure, continued weekly mentoring with Randy, and stepped into more of my strengths and passions. Professionally, 2004 had ended with me owning a window cleaning company, which soon expanded to include a handyman and small construction services. By the end of summer 2005, the construction company had grown so much that I had invited my parents to relocate close to us so that my dad could join me as a partner. This gave me some extra time to pursue my passions. Randy asked me to consider stepping into the leadership of the men's ministry at Adventure. After hearing God say yes, I accepted.

Fall 2005 through Winter 2006 I worked at construction and window cleaning and continued my involvement with the men's ministry at Adventure. We walked through a study on telling our story, understanding how the events in each of our back stories have shaped who we are as men today. I continued to pursue God, but I struggled to have a regular time with Him. It seemed like I went from retreat to retreat. Leaving one, feeling like I had been on a mountaintop, close to Him, hearing from Him, followed by a valley, a season of drought, waiting for the next encounter, the next recharge.

This ebb and flow of time with God also illustrates how freedom looked during this period. I do not have a lot of specific memories or journal entries from these months regarding porn and masturbation. I do know for sure that I did not masturbate during this time, which for me was a personal record. I'm sure none of you have ever kept track of your personal record, but my previous best had been just shy of three months. I celebrated as October 22nd passed and a new record was set. That continued through Spring 2006 and beyond. Resisting porn remained a struggle, a temptation always right there, always feeling like it was right underneath the surface, waiting to be found. Dream life was also challenging. In the past, I frequently had X-rated or worse dreams that did not involve my wife. During this time, those dreams returned with a vigor that seemed almost supernaturally prompted. I would wake up, shake off the bad dream, go back to sleep, and quickly find myself trying to wake up again, wake up out of a dream that I did not want to be in anymore. This was really hard to deal with. I thought I would be done with all this kind of stuff right away, but my subconscious was bringing to life all the garbage that I had carefully stored over the past decades.

What I perceived as my inability to deal with these dreams and the unwanted fantasies and thoughts they brought led to a lot of personal questioning and doubt. Questioning my own strength. Here I was, leading men at my church, and I couldn't even get my own thoughts under control. These dreams and thoughts weren't a nightly occurrence, but they happened often enough during those first six months after the island that I did start to wonder if my not wanting to be *that guy* was enough. Was it? Could that one decision carry me through a lifetime of freedom from porn and masturbation? Why wasn't it enough to rid me of these fantasies that I didn't even want? Self-doubt clouded my brain. But all the while those thoughts were swirling, some part of my heart knew I was on the right track. I had put so much garbage into my head, it was going to take a while to filter out. I knew I was where I was supposed to be, knew I was following God and continuing to hear from Him. But knowing all those things didn't always translate into a peaceful night's sleep.

The mentor program at Adventure was designed to take guys into the next step of their journey, whatever that was. As the point man for men's ministry, I had responsibility alongside Randy to lead this group on the same kind of retreats that had changed my life the year before. I found this responsibility incredibly intimidating. A lot of the guys at the church who were mentors had been walking with God longer than I had been alive. What did I have to say to them that they didn't already know? Randy and I spent weeks preparing for a weekend retreat for the mentors. Wanting to perform, to prove to them that I belonged brought quite a bit of stress in my life as I helped prepare the agenda. And at the last minute, Randy was unable to make it to the event. That left just me to lead. As I made the two-hour drive to retreat, I felt anxious and very alone.

Twelve of us gathered at a friend's cabin outside Leavenworth. Like most Adventure retreats, the format was simple. A brief talk followed by an extended time to seek out God, to inquire of Him, to listen. Saturday morning I headed out to find a rock to sit on, which was fast becoming my favorite perch for times with God. Crunching through the snow, I found the perfect rock for the day. It was sunny out, peaceful, an occasional chirping bird, the smell of wood smoke in the air. Praying and journaling, really feeling like I needed to hear from God. Deeply desiring to hear from Him. What was He thinking about my current state? Was He pleased? Did He like where I was? I worried that He was frustrated with my slow progress and my continued battles with temptation. For ninety minutes, I heard nothing. I was comfortable, warm, in a peaceful place, no cell phone ringing, no email dinging. But I wanted so much more. I wanted to hear from God.

I remember a kind of resolution forming in my heart. I felt God's presence in nature, around me, but I wanted to hear His voice. I remember saying, out loud, as if by speaking it I would believe it, "God, I'm just going to sit here until you meet me, no matter how long it takes." Here is what I wrote in my journal:

> I desire to have a large part in the story, Father. I feel your pull in my life that I am destined to do something great for your Kingdom. What is that? I ask that you speak to me about the WHAT, Father. I give you the HOW, all of it, all the self-reliance, the wounds, the messages, the baggage. I give it freely to you to carry on my behalf.

Since my dark years of the early 2000s, I had felt this strong but indecipherable sense that I was made for more. Have you ever felt that? Like you were born into the wrong story or the wrong play or maybe just born 150 years too late? Like you were made for the Old West, where right was right and wrong was wrong? I certainly did. And I didn't know what to do about that feeling except to ask God to speak to me. I did know that I had spent way too much time on my own plans and my own strategies for how to live life. But laying down that control and just listening to God terrified me.

And I was reminded of another fear – that I wasn't the right guy to lead these men. I felt this uncertainty so strongly that I wrote it down and asked God:

Am I a leader of men?

"Yes."

[Writing this book in 2010, remembering this exact moment, I can still recall the tone of God's voice. Only a few times in my life have I heard His voice that strongly and authoritatively. There was no doubt about Who was speaking. I was immediately, overcome with joy at hearing Him and felt a deep desire to hear more.]

So what should I be leading them in?

"Unbound."

[I wondered what that word meant, but before I could even form a question to ask, He continued:]

"A sexual purity ministry."

WHAT? This was out of left field. Immediately, I felt compelled to start writing down the ideas that were coming into my head. Bear in mind, at this point in my life I wasn't much of a journal kind of guy. But I literally could not stop writing. And four entire journal pages later, every core concept of the message of *Becoming Unbound* was written down. It was truly the coolest, biggest, most intense download I've ever received from the Lord. I remember hiking back down to the cabin in the snow, just stunned. As we went around the room sharing what God had spoken and what we were all going through, I remember being unusually inarticulate, as though I were unable to grasp everything that had just happened.

Excitement, passion, feeling God's love toward me and confidence in me. And what I wanted was more, more, more.

A couple months later I found myself in Colorado at a four-day men's retreat hosted by John Eldredge and the Ransomed Heart team. During the four days there were several times devoted to listening to God. As one of the sessions ended, each man left the meeting room with two questions to take to God: How do you see me as a man? Who am I in your eyes?

I made my way up the mountain behind camp, looking forward to just taking time, sitting quietly, listening to God. A couple hundred yards in, the perfect rock appeared. Bundling up my fleece against the chill April air, sun warming my back, I took out my journal and wrote. Excerpted here is a piece I wrote after about thirty minutes of fervently praying, deeply desiring to hear from God about who I am:

> "Lord, how do you see me as a man? I want to be strong, dangerous, a leader. Is that how you see me? Lord, is that what the final *Gladiator* scene was about?

[Earlier that morning I had completely lost it and was weeping uncontrollably during a clip of the final scene of the film *Gladiator*.]

> I want my life to have meant something, to have made a difference in the Kingdom battle [like Maximus]. Lord, what do you want to tell me?

> *"You are good."*

Another thirty minutes passed of my sitting quietly, waiting, and wanting more. Just a few minutes before our time was up, I (once again) internally resolved that I was not going to leave the rock until I heard more from Him. I wanted it so badly.

I want more, how does this conversation thing work?
I'm desperate for you!

[A picture popped into my head, seemingly from left field. It was an Old Testament sort of landscape, rocky outcroppings, an older man with flowing grey hair in a chariot, traveling across the desert. I first thought of Ben-Hur, followed by Elijah, but neither name resonated with my heart.]

> God, that is the second time I have felt like I heard the name Elijah. Is that right?

> *"No, it is not."*

> Okay, who do you see me as? Who am I like to you?

> *"Moses."*

Whoa. You've got to be kidding, right? I remember that moment in very specific relief, because the idea that God could view me like Moses seemed so ridiculous, so far-fetched, I actually laughed out loud as I said the word "Moses" in a questioning voice. And after feeling bad because I clearly startled the guy who was behind a bush about fifteen feet away – and neither of us knew the other was there – I tried to let those words sink in. All those thoughts passed in what seemed like a split second, and then I heard another sentence:

> *"Because you will lead my sons into freedom from slavery and bondage."*

Really? I mean, could God really see me like that? The former porn addict and ex-frequent masturbator as someone who would lead other men to freedom? Some part of my heart said, "Yes." Some part of me knew it was true. Not that I was actually Moses, but that my impact on the world for good through Christ could be big. God's plan for my life could be significant.

After that weekend, I began talking with Randy about a study for men called "Unbound." We decided to start with a five-week series in May based on the concepts God had shared with me on that rock in Leavenworth. The promo video that we showed on Sunday morning was twenty seconds of building music and one slide that simply said:

> Pornography and masturbation are bad words and should not be used in church.
>
> – Satan

The offer to men was simple – join Randy and me for a real conversation about things we don't usually talk about in church. Nearly fifty guys – out of the one hundred ten or so who attended Adventure – showed up. That study was remarkably similar to this book. I told my story, my journey from slavery to freedom. We talked for a while about how it actually happened, about what practical steps a guy could take after deciding that he didn't want to be in bondage anymore. And thankfully, blessedly, men encountered God. I could tell you at least thirty stories from that study. Many of them are men with whom I walk today and call my friends. Many of their stories are sprinkled throughout this book. What happened was amazing: breakthrough, freedom, transformation.

As summer rolled over to fall and into 2007, we held two more regional Unbound retreats. The offer was the same – join us for a real conversation about pornography and masturbation. And the response was the same. Sixty-five, seventy men showing up for a weekend retreat, really going to the heart of the matter with each other. In fact, the first night of the retreat stopped being just me telling my story and became each man telling his story. At the close of the first session, men were offered a chance to split into groups of three and answer these questions:

When was the first and last time you saw porn?

When was the first and last time you masturbated?

What would victory look like in this area of your life?

The first time we offered men a chance to do this, we were not really sure how it would go. After all, it's not a typical men's retreat conversation. But we often had to turn out the lights on the groups as they talked late into the night – most of them sharing for the very first time how this struggle had owned them. How they never had a place to talk about it. How they felt completely alone. How they had been convinced that they were the only one who ever struggled with this. All the same lies that I had believed almost my entire life. And more stories of freedom were born.

> Masturbation left me feeling weak and ashamed. I was never really sure if it was wrong or sinful, and it didn't seem clear from a biblical perspective either. Rationalizing it away wasn't enough to stop myself, and I thought it was just something I would always struggle with – even after getting married, and even after having children, despite the fear of getting caught in the act. This was the first time I was able to make a real decision to simply stop and believe wholeheartedly that this was clearly inappropriate and unnecessary behavior. Making this decision and change in my life has been incredibly freeing and also opened up new levels of openness with my wife.
>
> -Alan

Fast forward to 2010. I sit here in February, wondering why it has taken so long to write this book. It has seemed at times that Satan himself has been working against me finishing it. Even just finding one afternoon to write seems a monumental challenge. But my heart and the journey that I have taken to get where I am right now has been worth it. And the journey of your heart, the journey from where you find yourself today to where you would love to be in six months or six years...is worth it. So let us together switch gears. Let us move from my story to yours. In this next section, let's journey through not just my story, but what within my story made the difference in my life. Let's go deeper, together. Let's talk about what actually happened and why and when and where. And let's talk about how you can encounter God, experience transformation, and walk a life of freedom and victory.

PART II

7

THE PLAYING FIELD

O kay. So now you know where I came from. Maybe as you read my story you felt like I was telling yours. Maybe you identified with big chunks, with major themes of mine. Maybe you occasionally thought, "At least I didn't do that!" Or maybe you occasionally thought, "I wish I had gone only that far..." In any case, you're still reading. And that is a good thing. Because, quite honestly, there has probably been a lot of things going on in your life trying to stop you from getting to this next section of the book. Understanding where I came from is crucial so that you know a bit about me. But this next section is even more important as we dive into how I became Unbound. What changed for me, really? What happened to actually impact my day-to-day life in such a way that I experienced freedom instead of feeling enslaved? Is it just as hard for me to resist the temptation today as it was then? How did I tell my wife what was going on? Those are just a few of the questions we will answer together as we continue our journey of becoming Unbound.

Let's start by talking through some definitions to make sure we are all in agreement on several important concepts. One, none of these issues – sexual purity, addiction to pornography or masturbation, visiting prostitutes, child pornography, or whatever direction your desires took – none of these are salvation-level issues. I am confident that there will be many men in heaven who will look back on their earthly life with as much sadness and regret as heaven will allow because of their sexual impurities. I really do not want to be one of those men. And I know that neither do you. These are life issues. Jesus promised life to the full in John 10:10. My personal experience tells me that life to the full doesn't include porn and masturbation. But the question remains: Is looking at porn a sin? Is masturbating a sin?

The definition of pornography typically includes the usual outlets such as book, magazine, video, or the Internet. You should also include the porn stored in your mind. Your memories of all those things – your fantasy about the checkout girl or the latte girl or the girl walking by on the street on a sunny day. Whatever the form, pornography always contains one common element that is universally classified as sin in Scripture: lust. So I am going to assume that we can all agree that pornography in any form is a sin. But what about masturbation? The Bible doesn't really talk about it. It talks about wet dreams (more on that later), but it does not mention masturbation as a category. Many people have mistakenly interpreted the story of Onan as proof that masturbation is sin, but that is not contextually accurate.

> Then Judah said to Onan, "Lie with your brother's wife and fulfill your duty to her as a brother-in-law to produce offspring for your brother." But Onan knew that the offspring would not be his; so whenever he lay with his brother's wife, he spilled his semen on the ground

to keep from producing offspring for his brother. What he did was wicked in the LORD's sight; so He put him to death also.

(Genesis 38:8-10 NIV)

Onan withdrew from intercourse before he ejaculated. But his sin was not spilling his semen on the ground. His sin was violating the law. As author Mark Driscoll put it, "Using Onan's story to prove that masturbation is a sin would be the same as using Ecclesiastes to prove that it isn't."

Whatever your hand finds to do, do it with all your might...

(Ecc. 9:10 NIV)

The reason I believe masturbation is not specifically mentioned as a sin in Scripture is that sometimes it is a sin and sometimes it isn't. I do not believe you can make a reasonable argument that a six-year-old boy who masturbates *without lusting* is sinning. Just as a wife who masturbates her husband during a certain time of the month is not sinning. The way the modern church has interpreted the idea that masturbation may or may not be a sin is that it's okay to masturbate as long as a man is thinking about his wife. Unfortunately, starting with the best intentions does not equal finishing without sin. We men are visual creatures and are visually aroused. I have never spoken to or heard from a man who honestly did not think about arousing things while he masturbated. After I first saw pornography, I cannot recall ever masturbating without thinking about something arousing. The source does not really matter. Men who masturbate while conjuring up memories of past liaisons or fantasizing about new ones are lusting just the same as the man looking at Internet porn. I think you'll agree with me that whatever manner in which we start masturbating, however good our intentions are to not lust, it rarely ends without a degree of lust.

If you are married, the non-sin litmus test is even more difficult to hit. Genesis 2:24 and Ephesians 5:31-32 both speak of the oneness that sexual intimacy is intended to bring between man and wife. Is it reasonably possible to masturbate in isolation and feel closer to your wife? Even if you are able to masturbate without lusting? Intentions aside, that sounds extremely difficult. Military men and their wives have been challenged by this for decades. I have heard stories of wives who took revealing pictures of themselves and sent them to their husbands stationed far away. Do I think it is possible for that husband to masturbate while thinking solely of his wife? Yes. If he did, then I do not believe it would be sin. There are other examples of masturbation not being sin too. Perhaps you have experienced a situation where you masturbated and did not sin. I am not arguing that it is impossible; I am suggesting that it is highly unlikely. Years of conversations about this issue with hundreds of men have led me to the conclusion that regardless of our intentions when we start, for 99 percent of all men in 99 percent of all situations, masturbation ends up as sin.

8

THE BATTLE

wenty-five hundred years ago, Sun Tzu in *The Art of War* laid out five key components of warfare. One of the most crucial and overlooked keys is the idea of the Ground, the physical territory where the battle will occur. To paraphrase Sun Tzu, the combatant who knows the least about the battlefield will ultimately lose. In the battle for sexual purity in America, the ground has been very poorly defined. The at-large church in America has not served men very well in readying us for any component of the war we wage. Unfortunately, it has failed the greatest in helping us understand and define the Ground, the territory where this battle for freedom occurs in each of our lives.

The fact that we're even asking the question tells us that we do not understand the context of our battle for sexual purity and freedom. In keeping with *The Art of War,* let's use a military analogy to understand the fight. The war we find ourselves fighting is for our eternal lives. That is the big picture. The ultimate win or loss. Eternity forever in glory or eternity forever with weeping and gnashing of teeth. The war is for our soul. Assuming that your soul and mine will ultimately reside in eternity and glory, then this fight for sexual purity is simply one of many battles within the greater war. All of the truly saved, Christian men in America, have won, through Christ, the war for our souls. But we're losing the battle for real life, for life to the fullest, for freedom, and for all the treasures that God has in store for us because we're losing the battle for sexual purity and freedom.

The battle for freedom will last our lifetime, but each day can look very different. Sometimes a day looks like a few sniper shots in your direction, sometimes a full-blown ambush. Let's define each of these smaller battles as a skirmish. A skirmish is one single engagement with the enemy. One single moment in time, whether it's a simple chance to look away from the beautiful girl before you go to far or navigate through the checkout line magazine rack or walk away from an offer of adultery. A skirmish...one single engagement with the enemy. To recap: the war is for your soul, the battle is for your freedom, the skirmish is one single chance to choose strength. If your life has been anything like mine, this concept is a radical departure from the message we've heard our whole lives. Certainly that is not the message I hear from the church in America.

My friend Stephen was a pastor on the East Coast. He struggled for years with pornography and masturbation. And he has been quite candid about those struggles. A few years ago, he was interviewing for a new pastoral position and he disclosed his struggle. The board questioned him about his current habits and he replied he was experiencing a season of freedom. A while later, he had a rough day. He screwed up, in his own words, and looked where he shouldn't have. He confessed his sin to God, repented, and went back to work. Shortly afterward, he was called into an emergency board meeting. The church had found out about his mistake. He was not talked to, wasn't offered counseling, he was just fired. And it gets crazier. The board's next decision was to send a letter to the congregation explaining that he had been fired for looking at pornography.

Isn't that typical? If statistics are correct, more than half of the men in that congregation are struggling with porn on a daily basis – and that would include the men on the board. What kind of message would that letter send to those men...you look at porn, you get fired. Not exactly a safe place to have a real conversation as men. Thankfully, the board changed their mind and never sent the letter. But the message to my friend Stephen was as clear as the message to most men in the church – there is no room for even one mistake. Everyone else is perfect. You are the only one struggling with this. Shut up and don't talk about it or you'll be fired, cast out, or excommunicated.

Haven't you always felt that if you screwed up one time, all was lost? That just one mistake was enough evidence to pronounce the final verdict on you? I certainly felt that way. It seemed to be the story of my life. I would go without porn or masturbation for a week or two, maybe. My old record was eleven weeks! But somewhere in the back of my mind, I just knew that I would fail again at some point in the future. Another part of me knew that when I failed, I would just give up. Instead of picking myself up off the ground and getting ready to fight, I would give in and go on a binge lasting a few days or sometimes weeks.

This idea of the skirmish is not permission to screw up. It is not some kind of get-out-jail-free card that you can pull from your wallet when times are really hard. It's just the truth, exemplified in countless stories from the Bible of guys who screwed up, lost a skirmish, and still won the battle. Moses, Peter, King David – I mean, good grief, David saw a hot chick from his rooftop, seduced and slept with her, found out she was pregnant, tried to cover it up by bringing her husband home from the battlefield, then when that didn't work, *he had the guy killed.* And David is described in Acts 13:22 as a man after God's own heart. Is he described like that *because* he did those terrible things? Of course not, he is described like that *in spite of them.* He is described as a man after God's own heart *because those actions were not the truest thing about him.* And your past actions are not the truest thing about you. They are not the deepest thing about you. And they cannot define you unless you let them. The war is for your soul. The battle is for your freedom. A skirmish is one opportunity to choose strength. Winning one skirmish does not mean that you have won the battle. Nor does losing one skirmish mean you've lost the battle.

Sun Tzu understood that to win the battle, you must understand the Ground you are fighting on. Our fight, our battle for freedom takes place in each of our hearts. The heart is what God cares about more than anything else. He talks about it more than anything else. And when God talks about the heart, He's not talking about the muscle in our body keeping us alive. He is talking about the deepest, truest part in each of us. The part that reflects His image, the thing that will live forever, our soul, our deep heart. He tells us in Proverbs 4:23 that the heart is the "wellspring of life." The source from which all of our life is fed and watered and grown. The reason this concept of the skirmish is so crucial to our fight for freedom is that it redefines the Ground that we are fighting over. You see, our battle is not about perfection, men. We're not fighting to never screw up again –although that would be fantastic! No, we're fighting for our heart, for the heart that God has given each of us as men. The Ground, as Sun Tzu would call it, over which this battle for freedom is being fought is our deep heart.

You see, when you became a Christ follower, you were given a new heart:

> I will sprinkle clean water on you, and you will be clean; I will cleanse you from all your impurities and from all your idols. I will give you a new heart and put a new spirit in you; I will remove from you your heart of stone and give you a heart of flesh.
>
> (Ezekiel 36:25-26 NIV)

That is not a verse about sin management. That is a verse about a new identity. God promises to give us a new heart. That means you have a new heart! Period. It's new!

Why is it important for us to realize that we have a new heart? Because the old rules we have learned about this battle do not apply any more. Forget what you have been taught about sexual purity or how to achieve it. Understand that your heart is the deepest thing about you – and it is the thing God cares the most about. The core of who you really are is your heart. It is the combination of all your deepest desires, fears, and beliefs. Your heart is who you are, your identity. And it's the focal point, the Ground, of the battle.

9
D-Day

As we explore the Ground of our battle together more, we should also understand the timing of our individual battle. Like our own country's greatest triumph in war, your battle for freedom starts with a declaration of independence. Your personal war for eternity started with a D-Day. A declaration day. If you are a Christ follower, there was a day when you declared that God was in charge of your life. A day when you invited Jesus into your heart to be your ruler, leader, and friend. If you have not taken this step yet, but would like to, pray this simple prayer out loud:

> Jesus, I acknowledge that you died on the Cross to save me from sin and death and to restore my relationship with the Father. I now choose to receive that gift. I choose to turn away from my sins, my selfishness, and any part of my life that does not please you. I receive your forgiveness and I ask you to be the leader of my life. Help me become like you. Thank you. In Jesus' name I pray. Amen.

If you just prayed that prayer for the first time, welcome, brother! You have won a great victory this day for your eternal soul. The next step is the battle for your freedom. It starts with D-Day. While the battle cannot be won with a simple declaration, it cannot be fought or even started without one. If you are at a place in your life where you are ready to declare independence from sexual impurity, I invite you to pray this out loud:

> My dear Lord Jesus I come to you now to be restored in you, to be renewed in you, to receive your love and your life, and all the grace and mercy I so desperately need this day. I honor you as my Sovereign, and I surrender every aspect of my life totally and completely to you. I give you my spirit, soul, and body, my heart, mind, and will.
>
> Father, forgive my sins. I confess them to you now. I confess that I have struggled with pornography or masturbation or (other areas of struggle). Forgive me, Father. [Pause, take several deep breaths.] Father, I further reject the lie that I will always struggle with pornography or masturbation or (other areas of struggle). I receive the truth that I am a new creation, that my sins are forgiven, and that you are my new life. I receive that I have new life because of Jesus. I embrace that life and ask you, Lord, to take me deeper into this journey.

If you just prayed that prayer out loud, congratulations, brother! It is my great honor to be at war alongside you. Because after a declaration of war, we can begin the battle. But let me suggest one tactical piece of advice: please wait to tell your wife about D-Day. We will talk about how to do that, I promise. But not yet.

What better way to begin a military campaign than to put in front of you what you are fighting for. Why are you fighting this battle? Why do you want to? For at least a year after my D-Day, I believed that the battle I was fighting was the battle for sexual purity. Or the battle against impurity. I was focused on *not* looking at porn and *not* masturbating. It worked, but it was very difficult. Later in the book I'll talk about how it got easier, but suffice it to say that I realized later the real truth. This battle is not about managing your behavior or about managing how much you sin. *It is about real freedom.* That is likely a fundamental change from how you have thought about your struggle in the past. I always thought freedom would come from more self-control, but it is a far larger story than that. Freedom from the feeling that pornography is irresistible. Freedom to spend a summer day at the beach and not go home feeling like a dirty old man. Freedom to have a conversation with the coffee gal or the checkout gal and not even think about anything except looking her in the eye for the entire conversation. Freedom is about doing the things you've always dreamt about, engaging the deep passions of your heart, leading your family, raising your kids, being in a love relationship with your wife – and all the while feeling strong, feeling like a man, feeling powerful because you're on the journey of becoming Unbound. Your wife. Your children. Your family. Your life and the riches in Christ available here on earth. All this is what you are fighting for.

10

Your Enemy

ou know why you are fighting. Freedom. You know the Ground on which this battle rages. Your heart. You have entered the battle with your own personal D-Day. Well done! So who are you fighting? Understanding your enemy and his tactics against your heart is crucial to winning the fight for your freedom. We cannot talk about winning the battle for our own freedom without talking about who we are fighting. Once again, the modern church in America has failed us men woefully. When was the last time you heard a message about your sworn enemy and the tactics he uses against you? When was the last time you heard a message on Revelation 12:17?

> Then the dragon was enraged at the woman and went off to make war against the rest of her offspring – those who obey God's commandments and hold to the testimony of Jesus.
>
> (NIV)

Do we act like there is a dragon making war on us? Do we act like we live in a world at war with an enemy who wants to (take your pick) steal from us, kill us, destroy us, and devour us according to John 10:10 and 1 Peter 5:8? I certainly didn't act like that, not for most of my life. I believed in spiritual warfare as a principle. It was in the Bible, so it must be true, right? But it was reserved for really important people. Men who were actually dangerous. Pastors, maybe, but certainly not me.

How about Ephesians 6:12?

> For our struggle is not against flesh and blood, but against the rulers, against the authorities, against the powers of this dark world and against the spiritual forces of evil in the heavenly realms.
>
> (NIV)

Really? I mean, really? Our struggle is not against flesh and blood? Doesn't it feel as if flesh and blood is all that the battle has been about this whole time? Aren't the flesh and the blood the problem for us men? Yeah, this is a tough one to understand, for sure. I remember really believing for most of my life that getting control of my flesh and blood, getting it really under control, and maintaining that control was the answer. That seemed to be the very crux of the issue. And yet if we are to believe this verse, control over our own flesh and blood is not the answer.

The battle for freedom, for sexual purity, is a spiritual battle. It really is. Think about it this way: do you feel alive, do you feel dangerous for good, do you feel like a strong man after you look at pornography or masturbate? Of course not. So is it fair to say that you are not a powerful warrior for the kingdom of God if you are looking at porn or masturbating? If so, and if you agree with the countless verses in Scripture that talk about our enemy, don't you think Satan is extremely happy when you are struggling with porn and masturbation? Of course, right?! So isn't it logical that he wants you to struggle with this? He wants you to remain convinced you'll always struggle with this, that *deep down you are a weak, dirty, or different man.* Everything I just wrote is how I felt most of my life until I became Unbound. I remember feeling so powerless, like such a weak man. It felt as though I could barely get the strength together to give thanks before dinner. Prayer with my wife? Hardly ever. I just felt weak all the time. Winning this battle requires understanding your enemy, his tactics against you, and the tactics you can use to win. In other words...you must understand spiritual warfare.

I heard John Eldredge once say, "I had an epiphany the day I realized that not all the thoughts that come into my head are from me." Huh? Not all the thoughts that pop into your head are from you? How does that work? Let me share a story from my own life that you may identify with. I own a window cleaning company that also does gutter cleaning. A few years ago, I found myself on a very steep roof with a majestic view of the surrounding valley. It was a beautiful spring day in May, bright and sunny. I sat down on the ridge for a few minutes to enjoy the warmth. There was also quite a bit on my mind. My job involves lots of time spent in people's houses. Often the wife is home without the husband. I'd say 99 percent of the time, there is no awkwardness, just pleasant conversation and clean windows. But today had been a little different. Have you ever been in a situation where you knew you could have a woman? Not because of what she said, not because of anything she necessarily consciously did, just a feeling that she was available? That is the situation I found myself in. Now up to this point in my life, I had enjoyed sex with only one woman, my wife, Heather. And I certainly wasn't planning to have an affair that day. But something happens when you know you could. An interesting but toxic place for your mind to wander. So there I am, thirty-five feet in the air on this woman's roof. And this thought comes to mind: "You know, the story of Unbound would be a lot more powerful if you did have an affair."

Wow. The crazy part is that I remember not immediately discarding the idea. I mean, there is some truth to it, right? In some twisted way? The story of the guy who came home from Vietnam without a leg is at first glance more compelling than the story of the guy who *just* came home. But about a half second later, it dawned on me. *I did not think up that statement*. That did not come from *my* brain. The origin of that statement was most definitely not *my* heart. Mathew 7:16-18 reads:

> By their fruit you will recognize them. Do people pick grapes from thornbushes, or figs from thistles? Likewise every good tree bears good fruit, but a bad tree bears bad fruit. A good tree cannot bear bad fruit, and a bad tree cannot bear good fruit.
>
> (NIV)

Jesus was illustrating the idea that we can discern the source of something by looking at its end result, the fruit. We can judge the origin of a thought or idea by its conclusion. What will the idea produce if we take it to its full measure? Having an affair with that woman would have borne the fruit of pain, suffering, and betrayal along with who knows what kind of physical maladies. So, good fruit or bad fruit? Bad fruit. According to Scripture, that means there is reasonable doubt regarding the origin of the thought. I mean, really, does the kingdom of God stand to gain if I had believed and acted on that thought? No way! In fact, maybe if I act on it, what really happens is that I end up being convinced again that I'm just a *weak, dirty, different man who will always struggle* with sexual purity. The enemy would love that, wouldn't he?

As an aside…I'd wager most of you have experienced something similar. A season of freedom ending with casual sex. Jumping off the cliff of child porn – again. Another homosexual encounter. The weekend descent into download hell. What conclusions did you draw as a result of that bad decision? And are you still living with those conclusions about who you really are? More on this later…back to the rooftop.

So I chose to not believe the thought that Unbound would be a better ministry if I had an affair. In fact, I stood up on the ridge of the house on that gorgeous day, spread out my arms toward heaven, and said out loud:

"In the name and authority of Jesus Christ, I come against any kind of spiritual force of wickedness, any demonic activity directed toward me, any kind of spirit of temptation or lust and I rebuke you in the name and authority of Jesus Christ, and in His power I command you to leave and not return."

And do you know what happened? Whatever was there, trying to tempt me, trying to get me to believe something untrue, whatever that was…left. And I had a wonderful rest of the day.

Part of the battle you have entered is learning to be a spiritual warrior. After you finish this book, I would highly recommend Neil T. Anderson's paradigm-shifting book *The Bondage Breaker*. My approach to life, my outlook on life, and my interpretation of the world around me shifted drastically after reading that book. *The*

Daily Prayer by Ransomed Heart Ministries, found in Appendix B, has also influenced heavily the prayers found in this book.

I mentioned this earlier in the chapter, but it is worth repeating. The topic of spiritual warfare has been tragically forgotten by most of the modern church. My father went through seven years of graduate Bible school (going as a part-time student while he worked full time!) to receive his Master of Divinity degree and was offered no classes on spiritual warfare. And this was at one of the most respected theological schools in the country. My pastor, Randy, had the same experience in getting his M.Div. "Seven years of Bible school and seminary and not one class or lecture about spiritual warfare. Not one mention of the battle, how it works, how to win." The church today just doesn't talk about spiritual warfare. If you are like me, it may not be a familiar subject. Until now. Please don't hear me saying there is a demon under every rock or behind every bad decision. That every single bad event or choice is demonic. But re-read the New Testament. How many of Jesus' miracles involve the spiritual realm? One out of every three! Spiritual warfare *is* a big deal, and one which has been sorely neglected in our battle training.

The good news for our particular battle for freedom, for sexual purity, is that we have the victory on our side. Jesus Christ has *already* won the victory. We are the heirs to it. James 4:7-8 tells us that if you resist the enemy, he must flee. But here on earth, you must take action to take hold of the victory. Doing nothing means giving the enemy the win by default. You must act. You must resist. And so we will act together. Pray with me out loud right now.

Jesus, I also sincerely receive you as my authority and rule. I receive all the work and triumph of your ascension, through which you have judged Satan and cast him down, and you have disarmed his kingdom. All authority in heaven and on earth has been given to you, Jesus. You are worthy to receive all glory and honor, power and dominion, now and forevermore. And I have been given fullness in you, in your authority. I now take my place in your ascension, and in your throne, through which I have been raised with you to the right hand of the Father and established in your authority. I now bring the kingdom of God, and the authority, rule, and dominion of Jesus Christ over my life today, over my home, my household, my vehicles and finances, over all my kingdom and domain. I now bring the authority, rule, and dominion of the Lord Jesus Christ, and the fullness of the work of Christ, against Satan, against his kingdom, against every foul and unclean spirit come against me. I bind it all from me in the authority of the Lord Jesus Christ and in his Name.

Flip to Appendix B. This is a seriously powerful prayer. Yes, it's long. Yes, it works. Keep it with you for the next several days. See what happens. When you're hit with something unexpected or that takes you by surprise, just take a minute. Stop what you're doing, take a few moments for yourself out of the matrix, out of all that you are doing, out of your busyness and the complexity of your life. Just try this. Turn your phone off. Go somewhere away from your computer. For heaven's sake, just go sit in your car and don't turn it on or listen to the radio! Pray this prayer. Reset yourself and remember you who really are. Take notice of how you feel before and afterward.

11

UNDERSTANDING YOUR HEART

Understanding the enemy is the first step toward victory in this battle. The second step is to understand yourself. You know the capability of your enemy – you have been experiencing it your whole life, just as I have. Things happened to you that should never happen to a child of God. Lies were told to you...about God's heart toward you, about what God really thinks of you, and about your own deep heart, about who you really are. And these lies are critical in helping us as men understand what has been driving us toward pornography and masturbation. Because you have felt driven, haven't you? I remember the feeling I used to get a few minutes before I looked at porn. Just this sort of general acceptance that I might fight it for a few minutes, but that the desire was *fundamentally irresistible*. Nothing I could do would stop the desire. Maybe I'd make it a week or two weeks or two months or whatever, but I would not ever really be able to genuinely resist the desire to look at porn and masturbate.

To get to the heart of this, like all good stories, we must return to the beginning, the very beginning – Genesis. God created Adam but decided it wasn't good for him to be alone. So God took a rib from Adam and created Eve. And we've never recovered from that surgery. We're captivated by her, aren't we? Something about a woman, especially a naked woman, speaks to us about the heart of God, doesn't it? His wildness, His beauty, His mystery. William Blake said, "The naked woman's body is a portion of eternity too great for the eye of man." And we cannot get enough of her. The reason she is so irresistible and powerful is because her beauty, her mystery, and her wildness has a divine power. She is a picture of God, according to Genesis 1:24.

If you are reading this book, I can only assume that you've seen quite a few women's breasts over the course of your life. So why does looking at the next pair feel so irresistible? For all of us. Young men, middle-aged men, old men. Are you aware that the percentage of each age group that struggles with porn is about the same? What does that tell you about the nature of this battle? It's not about youth. It's not about place in life or level of happiness. Good grief, look at the stories in the recent media about sexual purity struggles. Men of power, politicians, movie stars, one of the most highly paid, most successful sports stars in the history of the world. At our core, we all share one common trait, a common chromosome. The Y. We are men.

> So God created man in his own image, in the image of God he created him...
> (Genesis 1:27 NIV)

God created us in His image. And how we experience life as masculine image-bearers of God must say something about God himself, right? Is it perhaps that He loves beauty? That He wants to drink deeply of it? That He has an unending, insatiable thirst for things lovely and mysterious and beautiful? Could that be it? Could it be that simple? Maybe that is why G.K. Chesterton once wrote, "Every man who knocks on the door of a brothel is looking for God." Songwriter Plumb said, "There's a God-shaped hole in each of us." Or maybe the truth is equally as simple and complex as U2 said: "And I still haven't found what I'm looking for." I do not have all the answers, but I do know a few things for sure. Men are created in God's image. Men are visual creatures by our very physiological design. Our desire for beauty is good. At its very core, our desire for the woman is good. Genesis 2:18 reveals, "The Lord God said: It is not good for the man to be alone…" So He gave us Eve. Then verse 24 says, "For this reason, a man will leave his father and mother and be united to his wife, and they will become one flesh."

If I'm understanding the sequence, man was alone and God said that was not good for him, so God created Eve. Adam woke up and said, "This is now bone of my bones, flesh of my flesh…" which I will paraphrase to something like "Wow. I like what I see." And then God said, "For this reason" a man will become one flesh with his wife. What reason? The only reason you can infer from the verse above is that Adam needed Eve. She was God's solution to the problem of man being alone. God rigged the world so that men would want women.

Let's say it again: Our desire for beauty, for the woman, is inherently good. Your desire for beauty is good. It reflects the heart of God in your masculine soul and His desire for beauty. I cannot remember how many times during the years I struggled I asked God to simply take away my desire. I have begged Him. Pleaded. "Father, just take it away," I have cried out in pain and frustration and heartbreak. Have you ever been there? I imagine so.

And what must God think about that request? I want to believe that His heart was genuinely sorry for our grief and pain, that His heart was genuinely hurt by our sin, but that our request was met with a fatherly shake of the head. "Take away the desire?" He might say, "But that would be like taking out of your heart a part of who I am." And I do not believe He will ever do that for any of us. Truly, the first thing we must realize about ourselves is that this battle for our freedom is about embracing our desire for beauty, not trying to push it underground. Your desire for beauty is good. It comes from your Father, the God of the Universe, who put it inside you as a reflection of His desire for beauty. It is not bad. But sometimes we take our desire in bad directions, which is what we should talk about next.

12

BURNING YOUR CARD

When I really try to remember the details of specific days that I went to porn or masturbation, I often end up with the same list of circumstances. Stress at work. Stress at home. That particular time of the month. A general feeling of inadequacy, feeling over my head about some project or assignment. Feeling like I had really screwed up at something, a relationship, a task. Often a feeling that my wife wasn't really taking care of me in the sex department. Sometimes more of a sense that she wasn't going to, so why not just take care of myself? You know, to help her out. The first time that I can recall ever realizing that porn or masturbation could help me feel better was as an adolescent. I was on a camping trip with my family, something that I looked forward to all year, our vacation together. Two weeks of time together, especially with my dad. As he was sitting in a chair reading one afternoon, I asked him to play darts with me. His response was perfectly reasonable, perfectly acceptable: "How about in a few minutes? I'd like to finish this chapter." But something inside my little boy's heart sank. I guess I wanted what every little boy wants, to have him leap off the chair in joy at the prospect of spending time with me. (In hindsight as a father now, I understand that he just wanted to finish the chapter.) But nonetheless, something pierced my heart in that moment. I recall walking toward my little pup tent, the heat of the day mixing with the salt of my tears. I zipped up the tent and the tears flowed.

I also recall a feeling in that moment. I don't know if it was just a sense that I had or a thought inside my head. But it felt like things would be better if I masturbated. Not that I even knew the word for it as an eleven-year-old. But something inside me at that moment became convinced that masturbation makes you feel better. Makes life somehow more bearable, more worth living. That you're able to cope with the difficult things when you know you've got this one special thing that is just for you, available any-time. When in trouble, you know where to go to feel better. My misery or sadness or loneliness could be erased and I could feel loved and cared for. And I believed that for most of the next fifteen years. Any time the chips were down, when I felt inadequate or unworthy or sad or really anything other than great, I knew that I could feel better – if only for a moment – by masturbating. So I did. A lot. It became my comfort, my place of solace.

In my teenage years, that feeling of comfort and solace was supplemented by porn. Looking at a naked woman made me feel wanted. It made me feel strong and masculine. We're men, right? When we have an erection, don't we feel powerful? And so for the vast majority of us, we've kept pornography and masturbation in our back pockets. Our own personal entitlement card. Wife not taking care of you? Pull out your card and take care of yourself, right? Things not going the way you want in your life? Pull out your card and take solace for a minute. *Find some beauty and some rest, some comfort and excitement, and feel alive again.* That is the offer the enemy makes each of us every day. The lie he tries to sell us. I bought it hook, line, and sinker for most of my life. If you're reading this book, my friend, you probably did too. But we do not have to buy into that lie any more. We don't have to play by his rules any more.

True freedom will require you to burn your entitlement card. You must give up the right that you have so long held dear, to masturbate and look at porn. Whether you've kept this entitlement card consciously or subconsciously, it needs to be burned. I mean, ask yourself, really – do you think that in certain situations you have *the right* to masturbate? I felt that way for almost my entire life. But just as we chose to embrace that right, we can also choose to say no. To tell our enemy that he can no longer take our freedom. For many of the men I've walked with, there has been an incredible symbolic significance in physically burning this card as well.

Find a lighter or matches, take this book with you and go outside.

Assuming you own this copy of the book, rip out one of the entitlement cards. Yes, really. Tear one of them out of the book. If you don't own the book, make a copy of the page. Either way, light the card on fire and pray out loud with me:

> Jesus, thank you for coming to ransom me with your own life. I love you, I worship you, I trust you. I give myself over to you, to be one with you in all things. And I receive all the work and all of the triumph of your cross, death, blood, and sacrifice for me, through which I am atoned for, ransomed, and transferred to your kingdom, my sin nature is removed, my heart is circumcised unto God, and every claim made against me is disarmed this day. I now take my place in your cross and death, through which I have died with you to sin, to my flesh, to the world, and to the evil one. I take up the cross and crucify my flesh with all its pride, arrogance, unbelief, and idolatry. I renounce my entitlement to pornography and masturbation or (other areas of struggle). I put off the old man. I ask you to apply to me the fullness of your cross, death, blood, and sacrifice. I receive it with thanks and give it total claim to my spirit, soul, and body, my heart, mind and will. I receive that I am no longer bound to pornography or masturbation or (other areas of struggle). I am no longer that guy who struggles. I am a new man, ransomed and chosen by Jesus Christ. I receive my new heart with thanks and ask you, Jesus, to take me deeper into this journey.

Good job, brother! I am so proud of you. Really. I am walking alongside you in this great battle for our freedom. You have taken the first steps. Well done. Let's take a minute to remember what we're fighting for. Real freedom. Not an accountability group. Not tips and tricks. Real freedom. What if you could genuinely not be that interested in porn anymore? What if you could genuinely not be that interested in masturbation anymore? Does that even seem possible? It is, friend. Freedom is available to you. The last time I masturbated was some time during the week before July 22, 2005, my D-Day. It's been five years since that day. And you know what? The idea of masturbating is almost comical to me at this point in my journey. (It *was not* like that in the beginning, when I first started on this journey, but more on that later.) But pornography isn't that interesting to me anymore. Do I have to watch my eyes? Absolutely. Do I occasionally lose a skirmish and not turn away from a movie scene quickly enough or look the wrong direction on a day at the beach? Sure. Does it define me anymore? Absolutely not. And from this day forward, it does not define you either. You are not a pervert. You are not a dirty man. You are not different. You are a brilliant and masculine son of the living God. An awesome reflection of Him as a man. And He is so proud of you. Well done.

13

HUNGER

So you've announced your independence from pornography and masturbation. Your very own personal D-Day. You've burned your card, your right, your entitlement, to look at pornography and to masturbate. Where we go next is to understand that what Chesterton said is true. We are looking for something when we knock on the door of a brothel, when we dial up that one memory, when we plan which website we'll visit at lunch. And if what U2 says is true, and I genuinely believe that it is, we still haven't found what we're looking for. After all, we were not created for this place. We were created like Adam, made for a perfect garden, a utopia, perfect community and a perfect relationship with God. And because of Adam's choice to walk away from God's leadership, we do not live in that perfection. We live in a world that is under the control of the evil one (1 John 5:19). So some part of our soul will always long for more. For a real relationship with God. For intimacy with God. For oneness and closeness with Him. We can taste that on earth, without question. But it is usually just a taste. For most of us, porn and masturbation have become a means to try to find another taste. But our hunger cannot be completely satisfied until we're truly in perfect communion with Him one day. Until that day, men, we'll be hungry. And being aware of our hunger, being aware of what we seek, is one of two things we must understand about ourselves in order to win this battle for freedom.

Remember when we talked about the kinds of circumstances in which you find yourself when the urge to masturbate is the strongest? Can you identify what you were really hungry for in that moment? Because I guarantee it wasn't about a naked woman. Stuff goes wrong at work. We get hungry and want to feel like we have what it takes to be a man, to come through in the clutch. When we don't feel like we're succeeding at work, we can feel more like a man while we masturbate. Can you relate to that? Or things are rough at home, kids aren't doing what they should, you and the wife aren't clicking on all cylinders...the anger, the frustration, the desire to feel in control...is any of this sounding familiar? I remember feeling pain and emptiness and not liking it. I remember just wanting to fill the empty places and relieve the pain. It always felt like looking at porn and masturbating did that, even if just for a brief moment. When I was feeling like a failure at work or at home, porn and masturbation called to me with an offer of comfort.

And in each case, I believed the lie from my enemy. I really believed that the naked woman or the masturbation was the answer. I believed that it would satisfy me, that it was what I was hungry for. But it never did satisfy. Invariably, within seconds of the deed being done, massive guilt and shame would set in. I'd feel like an even bigger loser. I'd vow never again to fall for that trap. And a few days later, the same cycle would repeat all over again. I didn't realize until later that what I really longed for in those moments was *my strength* as a man. To feel strong, to feel the strength of a true man like the heroes of my favorite films – General Hal Moore, Maximus, William Wallace. I thought that looking at pornography and masturbating would make me feel better, feel full, feel more like a man. But it never did. It always made me feel weaker.

Throughout those decades, I was never aware of my hunger. I had no idea what I was hungry for. I just knew that all of the sudden, the desire to look at porn and masturbate was overwhelming. And in the moment, in the swirl of past experience, faced with that seemingly irresistible temptation and the belief that I would inevitably fail, I would break down and choose to look. If you had asked me if it was a choice in those dark years, I would have fought valiantly with you to convince you that it was not a choice. Yet now I know that it was a choice, *rooted in the belief that porn and masturbation had what I needed*. It's easy when you are on the outside looking in to evaluate someone's addictions. Take your friend, for example, the guy who plays video games for hours on end. If you are the guy (like me) who doesn't really get video games, isn't it easy to see how he is looking for something in his life, and he has come to believe that it can be found in video games? Of course. My friend Dan said, "I remember the day I started to over eat. I was in third grade. My grandma put a plate down in front of me and said, 'Eat this, you'll feel better.'" From that day on, when Dan was feeling bad, he would eat, because he had started to believe that eating would make him feel better. It is that simple.

For me, porn and masturbation became like some kind of salve for a wound. When I was hurting, when I felt bad about myself, my situation or life in general, I turned to it to feel better. When I was feeling weak, it called to me like a siren, offering the illusion of strength. When did you become convinced that what you were looking for in life could be found in pornography and masturbation?

I don't know the exact date for me, but it feels like it was a long time ago. How about you? Could that really be true? Could you have decided somewhere along the line that life, real life, could be found in porn and masturbation? I know I did. Pray with me.

Jesus, I also sincerely receive you as my life, my holiness, and my strength, and I receive all the work and triumph of your resurrection, through which you have conquered sin and death and judgment. Death has no mastery over you, nor does any foul thing. And I have been raised with you to a new life, to live your life – dead to sin and alive to God. I now take my place in your resurrection and in your life, through which I am saved by your life. I reject the lie that true life can be found in pornography or masturbation. I receive the truth, that I reign in life through your life. I reject the lie that I will always struggle with these things. I receive the truth – that I am an heir to the things of your life – your humility, love, and forgiveness, your integrity in all things, your wisdom, discernment, and cunning, your strength, your joy, your union with the Father. I reject the lies I have believed about who I am in your sight. I receive the truth, that I individually was worth your sacrifice on the cross. I receive the truth, that I have the ability, through you, to choose strength in my daily life. Apply to me the fullness of your resurrection. I receive it with thanks and give it total claim to my spirit, soul, and body, my heart, mind, and will. I receive that I can *choose strength* every day and in every skirmish. Help me to remember that, Father, and take me deeper into this journey.

14

IDENTITY

The second thing we must understand about ourselves in order to win this battle is who we are. Who are you, really? Do you believe like I did that you are just *that guy* who will always struggle with porn? Ask yourself. Do you honestly believe the words I have written so far? Or is some part of you not sure if freedom is really available? What do you believe right now about who you are? Do you believe that you will ever masturbate again? Honestly? I remember feeling like that was such an impossible question I couldn't answer it. But I did know one thing for sure. I didn't want to be *that guy* anymore. No way! I was sick and tired of feeling weak, feeling like less of a man. So I stopped being *that guy*. And you can too. Let's talk about how.

It's one thing to have head knowledge of who you are. I grew up in the church, so I know the verses too. Romans 8, 1 John 4, and Galatians 2 talk about God's love for us, what He did for us, our inheritance in Him, and our true identity as Christ followers. My mind knew those things were true. But that head knowledge never really made it to my heart. I knew I was just a weak man without self-control. No one else struggled with these things. I was alone in my struggle and I always would be. How about you? A guy once said to me, "Ezra, you don't understand. I'm just different than the rest of the guys. I've got this kickin' sex drive. I'm doing my wife a favor by going to porn and masturbation." Can you hear what he is saying? Can you relate? *But I'm different! There is just something about me that isn't like the rest of the guys, so I'll just bear this burden silently. And I know that I'll always bear it.* Or maybe for you it sounds more condemning. Especially for those of you who were abused physically or sexually. *You are dirty. There is something wrong with you.*

In my experience, what we have believed about who we are as men generally falls into the categories of weak, dirty, or different. And of course the messages get reinforced when we do go to porn and masturbation. How many of you were abused as children and have ended up looking at child pornography? The message all your life may have been *pervert, pervert, pervert. Weak, weak, weak. Dirty, dirty, dirty. Different, different, different.* And you have probably believed it. Men, you are not alone. We have all taken on these false identities. We have all been told lies about who we really are. Somewhere along the way, we all started to believe them – and we thought the answer was in porn and masturbation. But to find the real answer, we need to know the question, right? And maybe the right question is not "Am I weak or am I different or am I dirty or am I a pervert?" Maybe the right question is "Who am I, really?"

For me, it took some time to begin to believe the truth about who I really am. As you know from my story, I grew up in the church. I sang the song with this verse hundreds of times: "Jesus loves me this I know, for the Bible tells me so." If you went to church as a kid, you probably sang it too. But in my life, as I struggled with porn and masturbation, the Bible "telling me so" meant absolutely nothing. When I heard God speak to my heart in the still, small voice and He told me, "I love you," it changed my life. Until that moment, I didn't really believe that was true. Sure, I believed the Bible was true and accurate. But life experience had led me to believe that the Bible had zero relevance in my life. It just wasn't real to me. I heard others talk about what it meant to them or what they learned from this passage or how it "spoke to them," and I simply could not relate. But after hearing God, that changed. I began to be able to relate to the Bible more. To understand what those people had really been talking about when they called it "God's Word" as if it really were alive. All those things put together began to change my perception of who I really was. And I found myself beginning to believe that maybe I was not just *that guy*. Maybe I was someone much different.

So who are you? Scripture tells us lots of things that are generally true about ourselves. But what about specifically? What do you think God thinks of you? Deep down, I had believed *for decades* that I was weak, dirty, and different. One prayer in a book wasn't going to change that kind of belief. Being aware that you're hungry, that you are looking for something is the first step. Understanding that porn and masturbation cannot sate that hunger or fill that search is the second. Understanding that God is the only one who can truly feed you, truly fill that void with real life is the next step. *But understanding that God can quench your thirst is not the same as experiencing His quenching your thirst!* I am not talking about some theoretical game or role-playing exercise. I am talking about God actually showing up in your life and changing the way you think about yourself. Did you even know that was possible? I sure didn't. Three decades in the church and no one ever told me that all the stories of people talking with God in the Bible were not just for the people in the Bible. They were examples of the kind of transformation that comes from encountering the Living God.

I have heard countless stories from men who have spent years in counseling, in therapy. Gaining knowledge about why they act the way they do. Gaining experience in managing that behavior. Understanding that what happened to them as a child changed their outlook on life and affects their actions even today. And I have heard countless stories of how one single phrase or sentence spoken from God to the quiet deep of their heart has done more transformation than the hundreds of hours they spent in counseling. Please hear me, men. Counseling can be valuable. Therapy can be helpful. But healing is better. Healing is the thing that gets you to freedom. And freedom is the reason Jesus came to earth:

> The Spirit of the Lord is on me, because he has anointed me to preach good news to the poor. He has sent me to proclaim freedom for the prisoners and recovery of sight for the blind, to release the oppressed, to proclaim the year of the Lord's favor.
>
> (Luke 4:18-19 NIV)

Transformation in your life, real change, is available. It is how the journey gets easier. It is how you can be truly free. Can you feel it? Can you taste it at all? Is your desire piqued? What if your whole life you thought you were dirty, that something was wrong with you – but what if God had a different opinion? What would happen in your life if He told you He thought you were like David? That you were a man after His own heart? Do you think that would radically change your belief system and behavior? I do. Because I have experienced exactly that. I believed for decades that my identity was *that guy* who would always struggle with porn and masturbation. But then God told me that in His eyes I was Moses. He told me that leading His sons from slavery into freedom was my mission. And those words from Him changed the course of my life forever. I was no longer *that guy*. I was transformed. Do you want those kinds of words from God? Because they are available.

The concept of identity is at the heart of transformation. Who you believe you are determines how you will act over the long term. If you believe, like I did for so many years, that *you are just a guy who will always struggle with porn and masturbation,* then you will always struggle with it. It is that simple. You cannot act in a manner inconsistent with the way you see yourself. At least, not for the long term. Anyone can just gut their way through something. A crash diet, an all-nighter, the last six months of a software development cycle, whatever. I had seasons of victory. But throughout each of them, I always believed deep down that I would return to defeat. Over time, you will always behave like the person you see yourself as. In fact, this is in my opinion the single greatest misstep that many programs have taken in helping men. Please hear me: I have no beef with AA or twelve-step programs in general. I believe that they have come from men with really good hearts who are genuinely trying to help other men. However, I do not believe that real freedom comes from changing your identity from *"that guy* who always struggles" to "My name is Ezra and I'm a sex addict." I'm sure that approach has worked at some level for thousands and thousands of guys over the years, but it is not real freedom. Real freedom is believing that it is possible for you to not struggle with this anymore. Real freedom is experiencing temptation from porn the same way you experience temptation to rob a bank to get more money. Yes, the idea of more money is interesting, but there are better ways to get it. Real freedom starts with hearing from God about who you really are.

If you are still reading, you are probably pretty tired of believing you are *that guy*. So let's stop believing it, then! Let's do it together. This is a prayer claiming your true identity. Claiming who you really are in Christ. Find a quiet place and pray this out loud with me. Imagine that you believe the words you are saying. Make an honest effort to believe these things about yourself as you speak these words:

> Holy Spirit, thank you for coming. I love you, I worship you, I trust you. I sincerely receive you and all the work and victory in Pentecost, through which you have come. You have clothed me with power from on high, sealed me in Christ. You have become my union with the Father and the Son, become the Spirit of truth in me, the life of God in me, my Counselor, Comforter, Strength, and Guide. I honor you as my Sovereign, and I yield every dimension of my spirit, soul, and body, my heart, mind, and will to you and you alone, to be filled with you, to walk in step with you in all things. Fill me afresh. Restore my union with the Father and the Son. Lead me in all truth, anoint me for all of my life and walk and calling, and lead me deeper into Jesus today. I receive you with thanks, and I give you total claim to my life.

> Father, I reject the lies I have believed about myself. I reject the lie that I am just *that guy* who will always struggle. I replace it with the truth. That I have been forgiven by you, ransomed by you, chosen by you, adopted by you, and that I am truly your son. I receive that I have all the rights and authority that come from being a son of the living God. Father, what do you want to say right now to your son? What do you think of me, Father? How do you see me as a man? I will now listen.

How did that go? I hope you heard something from God. Something powerful, something life changing, something that will transform the way you view yourself. Please take heart if you did not hear anything from God yet. Remember my story. Sometimes there are things in the way. We will cover a lot of these as the book continues. Remember, too, that sometimes God just wants to spend time with you. In my life, that is often the case. And sometimes, we just need more practice at listening and hearing God's voice. When my son was six years old, he asked me, "Dad, when we pray and ask God to speak, how do we get our thoughts to be quiet?" What a great question – one I am still working on a good answer to. Practice, a quiet place, a regular time, and persistence are the right answers, I think.

So stay with this. Make the prayer in Appendix B a part of your daily life. You will encounter God if you continue to choose to spend time pursuing Him and inquiring of Him each day.

15

ALLIES

So we've covered the battleground, warfare, your enemy and you, and your identity. What's next? Your allies. In this great battle for your freedom, you have three allies: God, your brothers around you, and Unbound Ministries. Let's start with the easy one first.

Unbound is a ministry built around men like you. Men who want to be truly free but have not yet tasted that freedom. Our passion is your freedom, your life. We are your allies. You can reach us through our website, email, letters, or simply by reading about our heart toward you in this book. We love to hear your stories. Write us and tell them. We would love to pray for you. And so would many others. But to do that, we have to hear from you. To tap into the power and support of your allies, you must take action. It is up to you to initiate a relationship with your allies. The best way to reach us is online at www.unboundministries. com. Please know that we really do want to hear your story and interact with you. This is not (at least not yet) a full-time job for me. So please be patient if you write to me directly. Okay, enough about Unbound Ministries.

Your fellow brothers can be tremendous allies. Let me take a brief aside and speak first to what an alliance with your brothers is not. It is not about accountability. Accountability is a wonderful principle, but the church often presents it as the solution to the problem instead of just a tool in the fight. We're going to talk a bunch more about accountability and how to use it later, but please understand that as we talk about alliances with brothers, we're talking about something far deeper than just accountability partners. In fact, I know men who would tell you that their alliances with brothers have saved their marriage, their relationships, and, in at least one case, their very life. Brotherhood may well be one of the most powerful assets you have to call upon in this fight for your freedom.

So how do you start an alliance if you don't have one? Good question. In the context of this battle, I think a great first step would be to give this book to a friend and have him read it. If you are both in a place to start your journey toward freedom together, so much the better. And perhaps the next step after that is to get together with him and pray through who you might invite into the alliance. Or give this book to a third guy. In Appendix C, you'll find a study guide for this book that includes thought-provoking questions you can answer as part of a larger group to go deeper into this journey of freedom. My personal experience is that the tightest alliances are usually mission-related. Something larger than each individual man brings all the men together to fight as one. A mission as large and powerful as freedom is a great place to start. An absolutely awesome second book to read together and discuss as a group would be John Eldredge's *Wild at Heart*. A companion study guide, the *Wild at Heart Field Manual*, is an incredible book to journey through with a small group of men – full of great questions that really help you get to know your own heart as well as the hearts of the men around you. One of the most powerful alliances with a group I have ever had was borne out of a year of going through the field manual, question by question, answer by answer, delving deeply into each man's story, each man's heart, each man's desires. That year was the first time in my life I felt I was actually making friends. Listening to another man share his life story and finding the freedom to share yours is true brotherhood. Start with one friend and the study guide at the back of the book (found in Appendix C). Your freedom is worth it!

So how do you use your alliance effectively? Start with the expectation that the brotherhood is not just about you. Genuinely caring about the other guys more than you care about getting your needs met will always result in your getting more out of the alliance. Too often I see groups of men who join together because they all want to get something instead of give something.

Compare this. Scenario one – you are in a small group of four guys. You know, deep down, that the reason each guy is there is to get help with his problem. When one of them calls you, it's because he wants something from you. Scenario two – you are in a small group of four guys. You know, deep down, that each guy in the group genuinely cares about you. That he'd come over to help you move. That you could call him at 1 a.m. to talk. And when he calls you, you know that he actually wants to know (for real) the answer to the question "How are you doing today?"

We all want groups of men around us like those in the second scenario. We all want to be known to be like that, to be pursued like that. And I think if we're honest with ourselves, we all want to help other men feel that same way. That's the beauty of a tight-knit group of men. When I think about my allies, I think of the HBO film *Band of Brothers*. The selflessness, the self-sacrifice, the willingness to do whatever it takes to fight for others – these are the qualities of a true alliance.

The next alliance we need to discuss is your alliance with God. Without question, it's the most powerful, most influential, and most difficult alliance to maintain. My friend and mentor, Randy, once told a story about a famous pastor, Charles Stanley, who came and spoke at his seminary one day:

> "I have only 30 minutes to tell you the most important thing you need to know as a pastor! The most important thing – hands down – is your daily, personal, intimate relationship with Jesus Christ. If you walk with Him every day, it will make all the difference in the world."

He didn't speak on theology or doctrine or formulas or techniques. He simply told the truth of his own life experience. Time with God was the only thing that kept him going, kept him really *alive*, not just living. For me, this means reading the Bible, spending dedicated chunks of time pursuing God, asking Him questions, spending time listening to Him, disengaging from the matrix, turning off all electronic devices, going for a walk outside. Space and time that allow me to be with God. Two books that have helped me develop an intimate, conversational relationship with God are *Walking with God* by John Eldredge and *Hearing God* by Dallas Willard.

I was never the guy who wrote things down, who journaled. But I am now. Why? Because when I started hearing from God, I wanted to remember what He said! It is as simple as that. And yet there are more pages written in my journal about recommitting to spending time with Him than any other topic by far. The self discipline of daily time with God is opposed by your enemy. Here is a quick test: Decide that tomorrow, just tomorrow morning, just for one day, you will get up twenty-five minutes early, find a quiet place in your house, and spend time with God. Notice what happens in your life after you make that decision. Do circumstances seem to be lining up to help you achieve your goal or making it more difficult? Do you think the enemy will be excited about you spending time with God? Of course not, right? Notice what happens to try to stop you from finding this time with God. When you get to the appointed time, sit down with a pen and your journal. Pray this prayer out loud:

> My dear Lord Jesus, I come to you now to be restored in you, to be renewed in you, to receive your love and your life and all the grace and mercy I so desperately need this day. I honor you as my Sovereign, and I surrender every aspect of my life totally and completely to you. I give you my spirit, soul, and body, my heart, mind, and will. I cover myself with your blood – my spirit, soul, and body, my heart, mind, and will. I ask your Holy Spirit to restore me in you, to renew me in you, and to lead me in this time of prayer. And in the name and authority of Jesus Christ, I command any foul thing, any demonic presence coming against me, and any voice other than the voice of the Lord Jesus Christ to be silent and go and not return! I bind you in the name and authority of Jesus Christ.

Now slowly read the verses below, very slowly. Let each word sift through your mind like an experience that you want to remember forever. Stop after each sentence or phrase and let your mind rest. Reflect on what it says, even if your reflection is one of admiration or wonder about God. Wow, He did that for me? Really, is that true, He loves me that much? Would He do that for me individually? Pay attention to your emotions. If something comes to mind unexpectedly, don't try to figure it out, just write a note in your journal. F or example: "When I read this, I felt so alone." Jot down a memory if one comes to mind. Capture on paper whatever you are experiencing.

Psalm 23 (NIV)

A psalm of David.

The LORD is my shepherd, I shall not be in want.

He makes me lie down in green pastures,
     He leads me beside quiet waters,

He restores my soul.
     He guides me in paths of righteousness
     for His name's sake.

Even though I walk
     through the valley of the shadow of death, [a]
     I will fear no evil,
     for You are with me;
     Your rod and Your staff,
     they comfort me.

You prepare a table before me
     in the presence of my enemies.
     You anoint my head with oil;
     my cup overflows.

Surely goodness and love will follow me
     all the days of my life,

and I will dwell in the house of the LORD forever.

When you are finished reading, pray this prayer out loud.

Lord, I desire to hear your voice. Speak to your son, Father. What do you want to talk about today? What question should I ask of you? I will now listen.

How do you feel? Pay attention to your heart right now. How does it feel compared to most mornings when you wake up? If your life is anything like mine, the seemingly eternal challenge is to just slightly delay turning on the computer and checking email. Or turning on the cell phone. Or reading the paper. Or watching the news. Or any of a thousand other little things that taken together steal true life from each of us. Think about it – how hard was it just to get up twenty-five minutes early? Did you make it the second time or third time or 487th time? It seems the same degree of difficulty every morning for me. Do not feel alone in your struggle with this area either, men. I am with you. Your brothers are with you.

I know with all my heart that God is with you. He wants to spend time with you. He loves it. You don't have to bring anything to Him. God once said to me, "You don't have to be productive, Ezra. Just come hang out with me." Holy cow. I'm still working on actually believing that. I'm a guy, right? Of course I want to be productive.

I used to approach God with this mentality: "Give me a job, God. I'll go knock it out of the park for you. Give me a task, I'll do it to perfection. Then I know I can come back to You and You'll be proud of me." Can you relate with that? But then God said, "Nah, I don't really want you to do anything for me right now; just come hang out." Wow. He likes me *that much*! He likes *you* that much!

In hindsight, my experience has led me to the conclusion that the primary tool to get really good at walking with God, at hearing His voice, at spending time with Him *is to actually just do those things*. Reading all the books in the world, developing the ultimate schedule to plan your time with God, finding the right prayer formula – all of those pale in effectiveness compared to just sitting down and going through an exercise like the one outlined above. A little time in the Word. A little prayer. A little silence, space, and a lot of listening. You will encounter God. I promise. You may not discern His presence or His voice without some practice, but I promise you that He will not withhold Himself from you. As James 4:8 says, "Come near to God and He will come near to you."

As we move toward the end of this chapter on alliances, know that your alliance with God is the one that has the power to change your life. It is the only real source to feed your soul's true hunger. My story may be inspiring – I hope it is. It might give you enough strength or will or passion to fight for a short period of time. But over the long haul, walking with God will ultimately be the thing giving you real life, driving your behavior, and transforming you back into the man that God intended when He thought you up – a strong, powerful man created in the image of God. The guy who has always been somewhere inside you. The guy God loves to spend time with. The man you were created to be.

PART III

16

CLEARING THE CACHE

This next section of the book is all about the practical. We're going to discuss telling your wife what has been going on, walking with your son in his struggles, steps to take to move forward, and some very practical armor that you can easily put on each day to help you win each and every skirmish in your battle for freedom.

Let's start with the most obvious – your porn cache. We all have some sort of stored pornography. Maybe it is a physical cache – some magazines or videos hidden away. For me it was a virtual cache. Everything from saved movies to saved pictures to memorized URLs and more. And for almost all of us, there is a mental cache. Our stored favorites. Always available and ready to be accessed in times of need. It is absolutely crucial that we deal with each of these areas as quickly as possible. But it is perhaps more crucial that we do not deal with them alone. Don't get me wrong. I know that your heart is good, that deep down you really want to get rid of the trash. I remember the feeling. And I really thought that

I could go it alone. But let me tell you from experience, it's just not a good idea in some situations. Like wanting to buy your wife something nice for Valentine's Day and going to Victoria's Secret by yourself to make the purchase. Not a wise decision. Why consciously walk into an ambush alone? If you know it could be an ambush, find another route or bring backup.

Finding another route often looks like a huge lifestyle change. I know a guy who literally cut the wire from his satellite dish to his TV. I loved hearing about that. I mean, if you struggle with watching the wrong thing late at night, find another route, right? Maybe for you it's canceling HBO or Cinemax or whatever. Go for it. And don't feel like you are weak by taking bold strokes, either. A very typical lie the enemy tries to feed us is that we don't need to act boldly. *Take it easy,* he'll say. *If you're really a new man, if you've really changed, shouldn't you just be able to resist the temptation?* What is the fruit of that thought? If it draws you closer and closer to sin without actually sinning, is that good or bad? I love watching my youngest son, who is two years old, figure out this kind of stuff. I tell him that the fireplace is hot. His natural inclination is to move closer to the fire, as if to make sure that yes, it is in fact hot. As a father, my goal is for him to move farther away, not closer, because I know that proximity to the heat can only increase the chances of being burned. Genesis 39:12 says that Potiphar's wife grabbed Joseph's cloak and said, "Come to bed with me!" and Joseph "...left his cloak in her hand and ran out of the house." Moral of the story? It is very honorable and correct to run, to find another route, to cancel DirecTV or cable or whatever it is that might tempt you closer to the fire.

Finding another route might be literal rather than metaphorical. You may need to change the route you drive to work or to customer XYZ's store or vendor 123's office. Old habits can be broken, but it's usually easier to break habits when you don't drive by the same place every day. "But it's the shortest way to get there," the part of your brain in charge of efficiency cries out. I know. I've been there. Trust me that there is great honor in driving an extra ten minutes to remove a temptation from your radar. And there may be a day in your future when driving that route is no longer an issue. But I guarantee that to win this battle, you are going to have to make small sacrifices in how you approach your life.

I was speaking with my friend, Greg, who has struggled with this stuff for years. He has been walking in freedom for about four years. He shared with me that one of the darkest days he had was a day where he drove his old route. He didn't go inside any shops, didn't buy anything. But he let himself go back to the old mind, the old ways of doing things – and that felt just as bad to him as if he had gone inside. Find another way, my friend, go another route. Your freedom is worth it.

Your cache might be the kind requiring backup. Mine was, but I didn't know it at the time. The cache in the computer was a tough one for me to clear. I know someone who threw his computer in the garbage. I'm not saying you need to do that. But his perspective was that the vast majority of time spent on that particular computer was spent in porn, so why keep it? I love that passion. I know just as well as you do that you can go through, delete files, clear the cache, delete browsing history, etc., etc., etc. We are going to talk through the mechanics of computer armor a bit later. The point of this paragraph is that it may not be the best plan for you to tackle this by yourself. It is a great place to call for backup because the process itself can be an ambush. It's simple enough, right? You highlight the file and delete it. And then you see the title. And you remember a bit about it. If you've gone to the trouble to save and hide it, maybe you remember a lot about it. Maybe it becomes a little harder to delete it. *Just one more time, a quick peek*, the voice in your head that is not from you says. *Delete all the others, just keep this one...you know... just in case.* Point made, I hope. Call someone you trust. Ask him to come over to your house or office or whatever. Walk through the process with an ally in your foxhole. It is absolutely worth it to protect your own heart.

Backup is also required for the old school cache. Burning your stash of magazines or DVDs or tapes absolutely requires backup. I once heard about a guy who had quite a collection of DVDs and had decided to get rid of them. So he had a garage sale! I am not joking. Trust me, regardless of your financial situation, God will look upon the destruction of this property as an act of great stewardship. I promise. But don't try to burn your stash alone. Just picking up the magazine and putting it in the fire will be difficult enough without the added adventure of trying not to look and think about what is inside. Find a buddy you trust, tell him what you are doing. It's just easier with another guy in your foxhole. And who knows? Maybe that buddy has been struggling with this and your call will invite him into his own journey toward freedom.

This next idea gets its own paragraph. Under no circumstances (repeat after me, "Under absolutely no circumstances – none, zero, nada, zilch") should you ask your wife to be your backup for any cache clearing. Do not do it. Stop considering it an option as of right now. Seriously – do not do it. Why? Let's just say that this is a case where my personal experience has led me to believe that this is one of the worst ideas ever. I promise we'll talk about it more in a chapter or two.

Some of you may also have difficult work situations to navigate. I once worked with a guy who closed most of his sales in strip clubs.

In his part of the country, that had become a cultural norm. He chose to radically change the way he approached his business, his customers, and his career. We will probably all face challenges like this during the course of our lives. In changing the way we approach the world, the way we approach our own sexuality, the way we think about ourselves, our lifestyles will naturally change, too. And often it will cause tension or outright stress in your workplace. If you show up tomorrow and ask the guys to take down that month's pinup girl, they are going to want to know why. And your answer from the heart will go a much longer way than beating around the bush and hemming and hawing. And know that you're probably going to take some ribbing about it. I'm also willing to bet that there will be at least one if not several other guys who are silently thanking you for your courage and bravery. You may become both the butt of jokes and the one others seek out for advice on this topic. I know, because this is what happened to me. The former alcoholic may "know" that he could go into a bar with a few friends and order a coke and be just fine. And he might be in a place in his life where he is really, genuinely fine to do that. But the likelihood of him being in that place very early in his journey toward freedom is remote. In other words, if you find yourself in a situation where the upside, the best case, is that it might not go badly, you should reevaluate that situation. There is almost certainly a better setting in which to put yourself as you fight for your freedom.

Winning this battle does not require cutting yourself off from the world. That is not what I'm saying and it won't work even if you did. But if what you really want is freedom, if what you really want is to feel strong and powerful and masculine, you may choose to make some changes in how you approach your daily life. I cannot tell you what those changes are going to be. But I can tell you that the men I have walked with in this battle for freedom have changed everything from carpools to TV subscriptions to computers to restaurants to driving routes to friends to careers. And to a man, they all said those sacrifices were worth the freedom it gave them. So take heart and do the things you need to do for your own heart without regard to what others may think.

Dealing with the mental cache is difficult. I remember throughout my years of struggling that the memories always seemed to be the thing I couldn't delete. These vary for each of us: memories of old girlfriends, movies we've seen, magazine pictures, whatever. The mind is an amazing catalogue, no doubt. How many of you can recall with crystal clarity that one scene from the R-rated movie the next day? The next week? The next month? For all of us men, the mental cache is also our world of fantasy – a strange combination of memories, of actual fantasy (things we would like to see or like to have happen), and spiritual warfare. Often a fantasy can take the form of the checkout girl or the coffee barista or the bank teller. You stop for an innocent cup of coffee, and without warning you find yourself thinking/day-dreaming/fantasizing about what that woman serving you really looks like without all those clothes. And quite often, the image that you end up with in your mind is some combination of truth based on images you've already seen and your imagination filling in the blanks. Add to that the spiritual warfare element, and suddenly you're feeling this amazingly strong urge to investigate further.

I've spoken with many guys who have experienced this phenomenon, followed by a seemingly irresistible urge to go look at porn and masturbate. For other guys, the direction they describe is almost like a meditative state, where that image just floats around in their head the whole day, just something to rest in, find comfort in whenever they need it. And still other guys have described a kind of subconscious effort to get more info. They will talk about finding themselves flirting with the girl or moving into her line the next day even if it's longer. Or just taking long looks, drinking her in the next time they are in the bank. Can you identify with any of those? I can. In fact, it's something I am aware of daily. The example of the girl in the bank happened to me last month. Innocent, right? Nothing happened, I didn't do anything wrong. I didn't even sin. But the desire to push the envelope, to drink in her beauty and find life in it was very strong.

Another facet of the mental cache is the dream world. I'm sure I'm not the only one who has had XXX-rated dreams before. Now, if you are having those kinds of dreams about your wife, awesome! But what do we do when they don't feature our wives? Mine didn't used to. They were usually replays of other images I had put into my head combined with fantasies featuring me. And usually lots of other women who were not my wife. Often, the spiritual world entered those dreams as well. I would wake up, knowing it was a dream, but feeling convicted that I had made a bad choice. Then all the old lies would come flooding back: "*You are just the same guy, Ezra. Nothing has changed. You'll never get over this stuff. Look, you even had a choice in the dream and you chose sin. Why keep fighting so hard?*" And on and on. So what do we do?

There are three steps in working through our mental caches. The first step is simple. We stop filling our minds with hundreds or thousands of images. The old phrase is "garbage in, garbage out." I like to call it the Tetris corollary. Go play Tetris for three hours in a row. Then go to bed. What will your dreams be full of? Stressfully twisting shapes, right? So this is a gradual process. As you stop filling your mind with images of porn every day, your brain will stop regularly accessing those areas of your memory. It will gradually fade away naturally. This is the same reason that changing a route is such a good idea. Or a job situation or whatever habit you have. *If you go to the same Starbucks every morning and the girl there reminds you of a past girlfriend, find another place to buy coffee!* It is a small choice that will lead to a life lived more fully.

The next step in clearing the mental cache is prayer. Romans 12:2 says that you can "...be transformed by the renewing of your mind." You can invite God to take the power out of the memories. He will actually cleanse the memories so that they no longer have the power to sexually arouse you. Of course, you can always choose to conjure up a memory and let it take you, but He can wash away the power of past memories. In my own journey, there were some very specific memories I felt had a certain power over me. Certain scenes played over and over and over in my head. I experienced a great deal of freedom by asking God to come into those memories and take away their power. Typically I would think of one specific memory and pray through it like this:

> Jesus, I come to you for the renewing of my mind. I desire transformation, Lord. I give you my every motive, thought, desire, dream, and fantasy. I give you my eyes, my brain, my body today. I submit all of me, every part, to you. I receive with thanks the work of Jesus Christ, his cross, his resurrection, and his ascension. I give you total claim over my life. I bring this memory to you, Jesus. I do not want it anymore. I surrender it to you. I reject any agreements I have made with my enemy about this memory. I reject and renounce any authority or influence I have given this memory in my life.
>
> In the name and authority of Jesus Christ, I command any force of evil, any wickedness associated with this memory to be silent and leave. You may no longer inhabit

my mind, my thoughts or my body. I resist you and bind you in the name and by the authority of Jesus Christ. Leave now and do not return!

You will probably need to pray through each memory individually like that. While I have talked to guys who have prayed generally about thoughts and had some success, most guys experienced freedom after praying through memories and thoughts one by one. Understand, too, that many of these memories have held sway in your mind for a long time. One prayer may not be enough to rid yourself of them. I have spoken with many men who went back again and again to specific memories that still seemed to hold power over them until the spell was broken. And to a man, they all said the time and energy and extra effort was worth the freedom it brought!

So, we've stopped filling our minds with garbage, and we've asked God to purify our thoughts and memories. The final step in freedom over these mental caches is to replace the bad with good. Just emptying the cache is not enough. I love the picture from the movie *Ghostbusters*. Don't try to think about nothing because you'll end up with the Stay Puft Marshmallow Man. Instead, fill your mind with the good stuff. The definition of good stuff will be different for each of you based on your individual situation. For married men, this is an awesome opportunity to really focus on your wife. Lust is a sin when it relates to giving yourself over to something you cannot have or do not own. Like your neighbor's car or your neighbor's wife. But your own wife? That is entirely a different matter. What do you think would happen to your sexual relationship with your wife if you spent three days thinking about your favorite physical features of her? I would bet that you will bring to her all your God-given desires and passions and it will be fantastic for your marriage. Not to mention that particular night. And this is not just okay, it's the way God intended it!

> ...and may you rejoice in the wife of your youth...may her breasts satisfy you always, may you ever be captivated by her love.
>
> (Proverbs 5:18-19 NIV)

As we discussed before, you were designed as a visual creature – all men are. So take that visually oriented desire in a good direction instead of a bad direction!

Single guys, sorry, that last part probably didn't help you clear your mental cache. But hopefully it gave you something to look forward to! I have a couple other ideas that might. And frankly, for guys who are divorced or separated, these ideas work great too. If you are anything like me, your office walls are pretty bare. What about investing in images that capture you? Pictures of your family. Landscapes that inspire you go to hiking. Sports that make you want to compete. Art that stirs your soul. Find pictures that take you in good directions and surround yourself with them. I am sitting right now in my friend Randy's office. His walls are covered with family photos and pictures of Indiana Jones. Adventure, Battle, Beauty. That is what we want, right? So go find what inspires you and invest in yourself to fill your mind with good directions. And ask yourself, what is the thing you want more of? Your strength or a temporary zing? Unmarried guys, what do you want more? To have a tiny taste of pleasure right now or the deep, soul satisfaction of saving yourself for the right woman?

The story I am going to tell you now is without question the most difficult I will have to put down in this entire book. When I got married, as you know, I was deep into pornography and masturbation.

Although Heather and I had waited until our wedding night to actually have sex, we certainly look back with regret on how far we did go up to that point. I remember the three-hour drive to our honeymoon location like it was yesterday. I felt such excitement and anticipation, the average speed I drove was probably ninety miles per hour. The night we had waited three and a half years for was finally here! Like many others (I assume) the first time wasn't exactly earth-shaking. More like what-the-heck-was-that? But that was not the worst part. The worst part was the memory of what was going through my head during that first time. And it wasn't anything about Heather. Here was my beautiful bride, offering herself to me. A picture of vulnerability, of beauty, of kindness, of tenderness, designed by God to be fully enjoyed by me. And I couldn't see her. I could not clear my mind of all the thousands of images I had stored there. Images of how things were supposed to go or what was supposed to happen next or what it was supposed to be like. And it was awful. So for you single guys, maybe what you want is *to not have a memory like that.* Maybe instead, in moments of temptation you can dream about what it will be like to sit on the edge of your bed with your wife and look her in the eye and tell her that you've waited just for her. That she is all you think about. It will be a beautiful thing, my friend.

We have one final cache to clear. The spiritual cache. Most of the men I have walked with have described in hindsight how much they had underestimated the effect that spiritual warfare had on this area of their life. As we talked about in the section on spiritual warfare, I highly recommend *The Bondage Breaker* by Neil Anderson, which thoroughly examines and gives a practical application of spiritual warfare. Winning the battle for freedom requires a clean spiritual cache. This is not necessarily about cleansing yourself from sin or repenting or confessing sins. Those are important parts of your own walk with God, but what we are talking about is specific spiritual warfare relating to your past experiences in the sexual world. Many of you have experienced horrific sexual sins in your life. Sexual abuse from parents, from siblings, from relatives. If you ever thought that you were alone in those things, by the way, know that *you are not*. I have not personally experienced them, but a *huge number* of men with whom I have walked did experience such acts. You are not alone. Know that. During those kinds of experiences, it is normal for some kind of spiritual warfare to take place. The spiritual oppression often attaches to your heart as a deep sense of shame (*there is something innately wrong with you*) or dirtiness (*you are foul, dirty, a pervert*) or unwantedness (*something about you is undesirable, unlikable, unlovable*). There are many different kinds of warfare; those are just a few examples. For those of you who struggle with child pornography (and there are a lot of you, I know) often the root cause is being abused as a child and the spiritual warfare that took root in that awful moment or moments.

For others of you, spiritual warfare is associated with past liaisons. The junior high girl or high school cheerleader or the young man on the corner. Past girlfriends, one-night stands, the prostitute. All of these have the same thing in common. When you interact sexually with another human being, a soul connection is formed.

> Do you not know that your bodies are members of Christ Himself? Shall I then take the members of Christ and unite them with a prostitute? Never! Do you not know that he who unites himself with a prostitute is one with her in body? For it is said, "The two will become one flesh."
> (1 Corinthians 6:16-16 NIV)

A memory is formed, yes. But becoming one flesh isn't just physical. A tie, a connection of souls is also established. And if the soul you connected to is vulnerable to any kind of demonic influence, you have exposed yourself to that demonic influence as well. And to be quite frank with you men, if you have past sexual experiences, what we know about the enemy and about women and sexual abuse virtually guarantees that they have experienced spiritual warfare in their past. And now you have exposed yourself to their spiritual warfare. I do not know what kind of consequences you have dealt with or are dealing with because of your past choices. Pregnancies, abortions, and STDs are terrible prices to pay for bad decisions. Birth control or other protection may have prevented some consequences in your story, but a condom cannot stop the spiritual warfare associated with sexual encounters. If the college girl you went too far with was abused by her father, it's likely she was dealing with some sort of spiritual warfare. Shame, maybe, or guilt, you can't know for sure. But what we do know for sure according to the verse above is that now you have been exposed to it as well.

Understand this: The enemy is always involved in spiritual warfare against you. He is the father and creator of every perversion in the world. In the Old Testament, the followers of Ashera killed their babies and placed them in pots outside the temple as worship. Today, we worship Ashera through abortion. If you were involved in an abortion in any way, you have worshipped Ashera. You have given part of your soul over to that god. It's not just a painful part of your back story. Your past liaisons aren't just memories. The spiritual warfare from those encounters is still with you and still affecting you if you have not cleared that cache. So let's do it right now. Find a quiet space somewhere in your life. Turn off anything electronic. You don't have to go on a hike, although that would probably be great. Just a quiet spot to park your car. Pray through this out loud:

> Jesus, I come to you for the renewing of my mind. I desire transformation. I give you my every motive, thought, desire, dream, and fantasy. I give you my eyes, my brain, my body today. I submit all of me, every part, to you. I receive with thanks the work of Jesus Christ, his cross, his resurrection and his ascension. I give you total claim over my life. I bring this past event, this liaison, this memory to you, Jesus. I do not want it anymore. I surrender it to you. I reject any agreements I have made with my enemy about this event. I reject and renounce any authority or influence I have given this event in my life. In the name and authority of Jesus Christ, I command any force of evil, any wickedness associated with this event to be silent and leave. You may no longer inhabit my mind, my thoughts or my body. Any demonic presence that has associated with this event, I come against you and I resist you and bind you in the name and by the authority of Jesus Christ. Leave now and do not return!

Good job, my brother. Well done. I am proud of you. When it comes to spiritual warfare, one thing that I have learned through experience is that it often gets worse before it gets better. Depending on your story, you may have a lot of work ahead of you in order to disconnect from all the spiritual warfare you have been exposed to. I would suggest making a list of all the sexual encounters you have had in your life. Pray through them with the prayer outlined above. Go through each one individually. You cannot just lump everything into one pot and clear it out. Clearing a cache has to be done one soul connection at a time. It is worth your time. Freedom awaits.

17
TELLING YOUR WIFE

What is the scariest thing you've thought about doing in years? Skydiving? No problem. Bungee-jumping? Easy. Base-jumping? Sure. Telling your wife that you've struggled with porn? Sheer terror. At least it was for me. And for many of you, the confession is much worse. Adultery, prostitution, long-term affairs. How in the world do we navigate this?

First of all, let me assure you that you do in fact need to tell your wife. We'll talk about when and where and all the other adverbs in this chapter. But you have to tell her. Your sin in pornography was against God. Confessing to Him is paramount and required. Your sin in masturbating was against God and against your wife. Confessing to Him *and* to her is paramount and required for healing and moving forward in your relationship. 1 John 1:7 says that "... if we walk in the light...we have fellowship with one another, and the blood of Jesus...purifies us from all sin." Confessing the sins you have committed against your wife and getting into the light and into a right relationship with her is crucial for your journey toward freedom.

I do not know how it is going to go when you tell your wife. I had shared with my wife, Heather, about my struggle with porn on a couple occasions. It was not a real confession, though. It was a weak attempt at not feeling quite so guilty about my actions. I did not share with her the extent of my struggles, I just shared that I messed up once and had a rough day with porn. She believed my transgressions were rare, not a broad pattern of behavior. She also has shared with me that she perceived me as a very weak man when I confessed to her, that I was confessing out of weakness and hopelessness, not a place of healing and strength. When I told my wife the whole story after the island retreat in 2005, the initial conversation went surprisingly smoothly. But as the weight of what I had done landed fully on her, there was a lot to deal with. It took six months for her to fully come to terms with the betrayal. And then it took another six months for her to see and believe the changes in my behavior. What finally convinced her that I had changed was when she actually experienced the change in how I related to her. I will never forget a conversation we had about a year after I first told her. She said, "You know how you are always saying that you want me to feel safe talking to you about anything? I think I'm finally starting to believe that."

That was about four years ago. Since then, we've had an absolutely amazing turnaround in our marriage. Before Unbound, I would have rated our marriage as maybe a 6 or 7 out of 10. We didn't have huge arguments. Things were generally okay between us. Compared to what we have now, our marriage was really more like a 2 or 3. I had no idea how what I was doing affected her. I now know. It was betrayal, it was devastating. My actions called into question everything she believed about herself and about our relationship. She thought I had messed up a few times. She had no idea I had been deeply addicted for those many years. But in looking back, I see how my belief that I was *that guy* robbed her of the man she desperately wanted and needed me to be. It helps to remember that for most women, the core questions of their heart are "Am I beautiful? Am I desirable? Is there something about me that draws you?" And you are going to answer that with a big loud "no" when you tell her that you have struggled with porn, masturbation, adultery, prostitution, or more.

All stories of telling one's wife don't go like mine. After much debate, my good friend, Joel decided to wait about six months to tell his wife. At the time, I recommended that he tell her right away, but in hindsight, I realize he knew his wife better than I did. Imagine that! His conversation was far simpler than mine was because he had six months of an established new track record. So as he shared with her, her reaction was more along the lines of "Oh, so that's what the difference has been these last few months." For her, it was easier to believe his heartfelt desire to change because he already had. Granted, there were still a lot of conversations working through just what that meant for her, but the track record of relational trust had already been built.

Another friend of mine, Jeff, describes the afternoon he told his wife as "...the start of the best conversation we've ever had." It opened up new doors for both of them to share deeply with each many other things they had never talked about before. And I also know stories where telling a wife went poorly for a guy. I think of one friend whose wife could not handle what he had told him. It took years for the damage to be restored, but restored it was. And their relationship now is better, deeper, stronger, and fuller than either of them ever dreamed it could be. So I tell you all these stories as tales of hope. It may not go smoothly, but it might. It may not go how you think it will. But in the end, the journey of healing that you will travel with your wife will result in a better marriage.

Let's get down to the details. We're guys, we like details, right? I'm not going to tell you what to say or put words in your mouth except about one thing. But here is my experience along with the experience of hundreds of guys about what worked and what did not work.

WHEN: My friend, Brian, was wrapping Christmas presents with his wife on December 24, 2006. She asked him, "Do you know what today is?" He replied in his patented Brian sarcastic voice, "Uhhhh…Christmas Eve?!?!" To which she responded, "No, today is the tenth anniversary of the day you told me you were addicted to porn." Ouch. Moral of the story…don't choose Christmas Eve as the day to tell her. The correct answer to the question "When is the best time to tell my wife?" is never. Because there is never a best time. You know yourself and your wife far better than I do. Perhaps you are like me and it will be important to tell her right away. Or you may identify more with my friend, Joel, who waited several months while his behavioral track record caught up to his new beliefs. Regardless of the timing, here is what I would use to guide you in picking out the setting.

LOCATION: Public places are bad, private places are good. Do not tell her in a restaurant. She needs to feel free to express herself fully and feel safe in doing so. If you have kids, get a sitter offsite and have the conversation with her at home.

SETTING: Unplug anything electronic. Trust me. Her mother will call in the middle of the conversation. Your work will have a pressing emergency. It is not worth the interruption for ANY reason. Do not have the kids around – at all. Watching TV downstairs, playing outside, working on the computer in their room – these are not acceptable. Ideally, they spend the night somewhere else. Plan for a minimum of two to three hours of uninterrupted time with your wife. More is better. In my experience walking with guys, the longer the first conversation is and the deeper that conversation goes for her, the shorter the overall time for healing will be. More on what to say in a minute.

HOW, Part 1: Pray, pray, pray. Pray for your wife, that she will hear your true heart when you tell her. Pray against the enemy, that he will be barred from the conversation. I suggest praying something like this out loud for several days prior to the conversation as well as just before it.

> In all that I now pray, I include (my wife and/or children, by name). Acting as their head, I bring them under your authority and covering, as I come under your authority and covering. I cover (wife and/or children, by name) with your blood – their spirit, soul, and body, their heart, mind, and will. I ask your Spirit to restore them in you, renew them in you, and apply to them all that I now pray on their behalf, acting as their head. I pray for my wife. Lord, give me the strength to say what I need to say and the compassion to understand my wife's reaction. Please allow her to see my heart towards her, my desire to be in right relationship with her. Please put the words in my mouth to communicate my true feelings for her in the moment. Protect her, Father. In the name and authority of Jesus Christ, I command any foul thing, any demonic presence, any force of the kingdom of darkness that is trying to come between me and my wife to be silent, leave, and do not return! Anything trying to plant seeds of doubt or disillusionment or drive a wedge between me

and my wife be silent, leave, and do not return! Anything trying to divide me and my wife, I command you in the name and authority of Jesus Christ to be silent and leave us alone! Go now and do not return! Father, summon your angels to stand watch over me, my house, and my wife as I prepare to talk with her.

HOW, Part 2: Be as brief as possible. What she needs to know is that you messed up really badly and that you are sorry about those bad decisions. Tell her the overview of what you have done, but *absolutely do not, I repeat, do not* go into details. In other words, she needs to know that you have struggled with pornography for the last twelve years. She does not need to know that you routinely go to Shop XYZ to look at videos. This is not hiding anything from her but staying focused on the issue. If you have had sex outside marriage, she needs to know. She needs to know if it was a one-time mistake or if it happened a lot. But a list of names, details, and places will not help her heal faster. The exception to this guideline is in future conversations. In my story, HBO and other late night cable programs were often a struggle for me. I was (later) able to share that fact when we were talking about giving up TV – which, by the way, I highly recommend, especially the one in the master bedroom.

I hope this makes sense, men. You are not trying to hide anything from your wife. It has been my experience and that of many other men that the gory details only hurt her and distract from the main issue. Again, she has a right to know if you've had sex with a prostitute. There is going to be an incredible amount of pain there, along with questions about health, STDs, etc. Let those questions come from her. You don't need to volunteer the "good news" that you did not get any STDs from those encounters. She may not have even considered that yet. If you have struggled with child pornography, you may have some very serious challenges to navigate, including legal action against you. But it is probably not going to be helpful during the first conversation to try to talk through that with her. Remember, she will probably not understand why this is an issue for you. No matter what you say, she will most likely come to the conclusion that you weren't happy with her as a woman, so you looked elsewhere. Details about the looking won't help her get to the truth – that you were wrong and that you are sorry. So let her lead the conversation; answer her questions honestly and concisely and keep pursuing her heart during the whole process.

HOW, Part 3: After you tell her, stop talking. I am not joking. The best possible posture you can take after you tell her what you've done is to sit back with zero defense and just take everything that comes your way. She may be pissed. She may have all kinds of questions and accusations. DO NOT rationalize your behavior. DO NOT make any excuses. DO NOT (please, please, please repeat after me...DO NOT) promise that you will never do it again. DO NOT ask for forgiveness. You are not in a position to ask for anything at all during this conversation. DO NOT defend yourself at all. Be prepared for her to be furious and heartbroken all at once. She may come at you with a thousand different verbal missiles. Be strong. Take them all. No excuses. No defense. Her anger at you is good, as it helps her get to the pain. In fact, these six words are the best and most helpful words that can come out of your mouth after your initial confession. This is the one time I'm going to tell you what to say. I'm actually so serious about this that I put these magic six words on their own page.

I was wrong.

I am sorry.

Men, that is the truth of what she most needs to hear during this first conversation. That you really were wrong. And that you really are sorry. No amount of explaining can help her right now. In fact, everything you may understand about yourself after reading this book – your desires, why you turn to porn, your new heart, your D-Day, etc., etc., etc. – none of that means anything to her until she sees it bearing fruit in your life. Otherwise it's just words. You cannot convince her during this first conversation that you will change or that you are changed. She will have to see it to believe it. And that is also why you should not ask her for forgiveness yet. Her pain may take some time to work through. Don't short-circuit her healing process. I know, because I made this mistake during the first conversation with Heather. I asked her to forgive me and she said yes. In hindsight, it was clearly a yes out of obligation. And that delayed her from really being able to forgive me. In fact, it wasn't until about six months later that Heather said to me, "I think I'm ready to forgive you for betraying me for the first ten years of our marriage."

As you are absorbing everything she says and responding with "I was wrong and I am sorry," be aware of her. Ask her questions like "How are feeling about all this?" Especially if she is not telling you already. Pursue her heart with open-ended questions. You've got to get her talking about how she is feeling. It may not be pretty, but getting all that emotion out into the open will lay a strong foundation for the future. When she starts yelling at you, shove your anger down inside. It's not righteous anger, trust me. Regardless of the role she has played in your bad decisions, now is not the time to talk about that. It is solely the time for her to be heard by you. DO NOT bring up anything about her during this conversation. Regardless of the truth, she probably cannot hear it. It will sound like you are being defensive and trying to blame her for your screw-ups. Pursue her, tell her that you were wrong, and apologize.

Lastly, read Appendix A of this book. This is a letter written by my wife to your woman. It may not make perfect sense to you, but that is okay. It wasn't written specifically for you. It was written to help your wife navigate through the most difficult part of hearing that you have struggled – taking it personally. Because sexuality is so personal and intimate, most women immediately draw the conclusion that their husband's struggle with porn and masturbation was caused by some failure on their part as a wife or a woman. As you know now, this is absolutely not true. You should read those words so that you understand what it will be like for her. But do not quote them to her. Those words are not designed to be your evidence of how she should act or how she should process the bad decisions you have made. Those words were written for her ears to hear. Give her this book and ask her to read Appendix A after your first conversation with her.

Final thoughts about telling your wife. You can do this. I know that you can. Whatever the current state of your relationship with your wife, she is the right woman for you. No matter what has happened, no matter what she has done, no matter what you have done, she is the right woman for you. And more importantly for you, you are the right man for her. You are literally the only man on earth who can fight for her the way she needs to be fought for and love her the way she needs to be loved. The truth is that you really are the man for her. She needs you. You have what it takes to come through for her. To really be the man that she needs and wants and desires. And believe me, men, whatever it takes, however long it takes, whatever steps need to be accomplished are all worth the relationship that is waiting for you on the other end – one of deep, soul-satisfying connection. Of a life actually lived together instead of just alongside one another. And let's not forget…the best sex ever! So take heart, find your courage, choose strength, and reap the rewards.

18

WALKING WITH YOUR SON

"And as I hung up the phone it occurred to me,
He'd grown up just like me, my boy was just like me."
"Cat's in the Cradle" by Harry Chapin

What do you really want for your son?

Sit with that thought for just a moment. Move beyond the usual trite answers – happiness, success, a good wife, whatever. How do you want his life to be different from yours? Isn't that the question behind the question that most of us dads are trying to answer? What about this part of his journey? How do you want his journey with porn and masturbation and whatever else to be different than yours? My heart breaks as I think about this question. My older son is seven years old and there is already a message in my head somewhere that *I have blown it.* And somewhere deeper there is another message – *not only have I blown it, but that ground is never recoverable.* Do you hear that message? Well, it is a lie straight from the pit of hell. Say this out loud with me right now:

"In the name and authority of Jesus Christ, I renounce the idea that I have blown it with my son. I receive the resurrection of Jesus Christ as my new life. I receive the truth that my heart is new and good. I receive the truth that it is not too late to start a deeper relationship with my son."

Every single man I have ever talked to about this in my entire life has heard this lie about his relationship with his son. Every. Single. One. This is a significant and universal method the enemy uses to try to divide and conquer fathers and sons. It is a lie. In the same way that you are the only man for your wife, you are the only father for your son. Regardless of whether he is seven or twenty-seven or forty-seven. Regardless of whether or not you currently have a relationship with him. Regardless of whether or not you are still married to his mother. He desperately needs and wants your involvement in his life. But he may not be showing you that. If, like the song "Cat's in the Cradle," your life and relationship with him has seemed to slip by, you may have more work to do in rebuilding your relationship with him. But it is not too late. To prove this, check your own heart about your father. It's entirely possible that your father was or still is a nightmare. Maybe you have spent the last forty years building walls of protection around your heart because of how much his influence in your life has hurt you. First, let me say that I'm sorry that happened to you. If you had that sort of dad, is it possible for you to think theoretically about fathers for a minute? What would you have loved for him to do? What memories would you love to have about him and you? Imagine with me for a moment. What if your phone rang right now? And after you said, "Hello," what if you heard your father's voice, shaking with emotion, on the other end. "Son, I didn't tell you this enough when you were young. I love you. I am so proud of you. You are the best son a father could ever have." What would your heart do with that? Isn't that what all men want to hear from their father?

What would absolutely knock your socks off if your dad did it? Call you and say something like the example above? Write a few thoughts down that come to mind. Allow yourself to dream – what would that look like? "I wish we had worked on cars more together" or "I wish he had worked on cars less" or "I wish he had taught me more about fishing" or "I wish he hadn't worked so much," etc., etc. My experience in talking with men about what they wish their dads had done differently has brought me to one general conclusion. What a boy really wants is for his dad to be interested in what the boy is interested in. The boy will spend time doing whatever dad is doing if the right relationship is there, but what really speaks the love of God into the boy is for the dad to invest in *what the boy wants to do*. Do you see this with your son?

Recently I have been in a phase of life, as John Eldredge would put it, of learning how to be a cowboy. Not literally learning how to ride horses or herd cattle, but instead of taking broken things to the repair shop, I'm trying to fix them myself. Learning how to be more self-reliant, able to be trusted with lots of different kinds of tasks, able to figure out how to do things. Like a cowboy who would be sent out for the day, not knowing what he might face, but comfortable in his own abilities to deal with whatever came his way. So recently, my son, Isaac, who is seven, and I have been fixing stuff. His battery-powered, ride-around tractor broke, so we ordered parts, totally disassembled the tractor, and rebuilt it. And it works! The pull string for the weed-whacker broke, so we took it apart, figured out the problem, and replaced the necessary parts. And it works! And in all those fun times of dirty, greasy, oily hands and wrenches and screwdrivers, I think I realized something pretty big. I was doing those things for me. Not for Isaac. He was with me, I think he had fun, but to be honest, I probably didn't let him do enough of the wrenching and screwing and actual work. In the end, I believe he did have a good time just hanging out with me. And he is certainly enjoying the benefit of the fixed tractor. But if my goal had been to build a relationship with him, if my goal had been "I'm going to do whatever it takes with the next two hours to end up with a stronger, closer, tighter, more trusting relationship with my son," I would have played Legos with him.

Men, do you see it? What my son desperately wants is *me* engaging as *me* in *his* world. That speaks to him that I love his life, that I want to be with him in what he is doing and I'm not just content to have him tag along with me. Now certainly as boys become young men, they want to be invited into a man's world and initiated into masculinity. But they will still crave the dad who engages with them at their level, who wants to know about them, who pursues them, who still wants to play Legos with them. Think about this. If your dad is still alive and in relationship with you, what do you really want when you tell him a story about a something that went great recently in your life? Do you want him to one-up you with a story from his life? Do you want him to quickly change the subject because he is embarrassed about his own life? Do you want him to give you some advice about how to do even better next time? Or do you want him to be genuinely excited and proud of you and tell you that he is proud of you and that he loves you? Do you want him to engage with you, ask you questions about how you did it, how it happened? Yeah, deep down, we just want our dads to play Legos with us.

So what does all that have to do with walking with your son in his journey of pornography and masturbation? Let's go back to what you really want for him. For me personally, my great desire for my son is that he does not have to go through the pain that I did in my own journey of bad decisions about porn and masturbation. In the last few months of tractor-fixing realizations, what has dawned on me is that I cannot tell him what to do when it comes to porn and masturbation. It is a journey every boy, every young man, every man must walk for himself. But like my relationship with him, what I can do is *meet him where he is* and walk alongside him. Not a lecture. Not a litany of what to do and what not to do. Not guilt. Not shame. A shared journey. Men, imagine how awesome this could be! I have this dream where Isaac is seventeen, and we are talking about how things are going with masturbation. He is asking me questions about what does he do when such-and-such happens, or he likes this girl and thinks about her, or he had a rough day and looked at a movie cover and couldn't get it out of his head and screwed up and masturbated and what now?!?! I don't know how that strikes you, but chills are running up and down my spine as I type these words. What an absolutely amazing relationship to have with my son. I want that – don't you want that with yours?

I'm convinced that we can have that kind of relationship with our sons, regardless of where we are right now. It may take months or years or decades, but men, it is available to us. In the same way that kind of relationship is available with our true heavenly Father. Even if we've waited to approach Him for a long time, isn't He always ready to listen and spend time with us? Absolutely. He loves talking with us about our lives, about our hopes and dreams and what is going on with us. So how do we get there with our sons? The answer is both encouragingly simple and discouragingly difficult. Time. I find it so difficult to make Lego time a priority. There always seems to be another choice that makes more sense. Returning a phone call. Checking email. Paying bills.

Whatever. I don't have this all figured out; I am on the journey. But I am becoming convinced that every little decision I make to not spend Lego time adds a brick to the relational divide between me and my son. And every chunk of time I spend with him is like a bulldozer destroying whatever is coming between us. It seems like there are weeks and months where a lot of bricks get mortared in and getting into the bulldozer seems so difficult. I mean, really, how hard is it to actually find a chunk of good-quality time to spend with your son? Not shopping at the Home Depot. Not doing something you want to do and dragging him along. But doing what he wants to do. Really engaging with him. If we can somehow figure out how to do that regularly, we will have the building blocks of trust necessary to move forward in walking with him in his journey. I am realizing in my own life that the first step in discussing porn and masturbation with my son is to be in a relationship with him where we have a deep level of trust and openness. If you do not have that level of relationship with your son yet, don't start talking with him about things that require deep intimacy. Build the relationship, then talk. Otherwise it's *just* talk and he will absolutely know it.

There seems to be a couple really significant areas for us fathers that get in the way of this kind of relationship with our sons. Shame, guilt, discomfort, and unease about the topic are big ones. Hopefully by the end of this book you have dealt with most of those, but the point remains. You cannot have a meaningful conversation with your son about porn without being comfortable in your own journey with porn. You cannot talk to your son about masturbation if you still feel like a dirty pervert. He'll know it's just talk. You absolutely do not need to be finished with the journey, because that would mean you are dead. In fact, to be a great mentor just means that you are a half step ahead of someone on the journey. No more is required. A half step. Just enough forward vision to shed light on the next move. You do not have to have all the answers. In fact, most dads I've met who *do* have a lot of answers became frustrated when they tried to solve a problem instead of just walking with their son.

I have a great relationship with my dad. Today, we are father and son, brothers, partners, and friends. When I was a young boy, much like my own experience as the father of a young boy, he got into situations where he did not know the answer. The conversations I had with my dad about masturbation before I was a teenager are encapsulated by one single Saturday morning that I'll always remember.

I was about six years old, squirming around under the covers. My dad came into the room and asked me what I was doing. In innocence I told him that I was touching myself because it felt good. His response was "Don't do that. We'll talk about why when you are older." I know my dad's heart toward me was very good in that moment. He just did not know how to handle that situation. The conclusion that my enemy helped me come to in that moment was that I shouldn't talk about it anymore. And I didn't, for a very long time. I realize now that what I wanted in that moment was to be walked alongside of, not answered. The same applies to your son. Think about how you have wrestled with the idea that you could be a good man and a Christian and still struggle with this stuff. Isn't it possible that your son feels the same way? The raging hormone-infused, teenage Christian young man. Knowing God, but feeling like he is unable to stop looking. Does he want you to tell him to stop? Of course not! Was it ever helpful in your journey when someone else told you to just stop doing that because your body was a temple, blah, blah, blah? Of course not!

What your boy really wants is the same thing you want. Shared time, shared experiences, being walking with, being trusted, being pursued. I envision a weekly conversation with my son: How has it been going this week with porn? With masturbation? I pray that he feels the freedom to come to me and tell me when he has screwed up. Knowing that I won't preach to him, knowing that I will ask him questions about how he was feeling and what he was hungry for and how he felt afterward and did he come to any conclusions about himself that are untrue? And knowing also that I'll then pray for him. Not a "Jesus help me" prayer but a fierce warrior prayer of repentance and renouncing agreements and fighting with all my heart and all my strength for my son. Not shame, not guilt, but a shared journey. I dream about that with Isaac and Judah, my boys. That is what I really want for them and for me. It is a beautiful picture, isn't it? The picture of your personal relationship with God, mirrored in your personal relationship with your son. A relationship of journeying together, of increasing intimacy and trust. A safe place, where when we screw up, there is forgiveness and the opportunity for learning and growth instead of condemnation.

As you begin growing your relationship with your son and walking with him in his journey, I think the greatest challenge to your son's purity is the culture in which he is growing up. According to Focus on the Family research, the average age when a boy first sees pornography has gone down from eleven years old in 1998 to five years old in 2005. Accidentally, of course, just doing homework or playing games on the Internet. But it is everywhere, always looking to hook another one. If your teenager is an average American teen, he is spending nearly eight hours daily being influenced by cultural media, including music, TV, movies, social media websites, and texting. Do you know what sexting is yet?

Please don't Google it right now. It is the practice of girls taking revealing pictures of themselves and sending them to others via their cell phone. Somewhere, somehow, our culture has slowly been removing barriers to sexuality. Did you know that less than 3 percent of males wait until marriage to have sex? That less than 1 percent of all marriages start with virginity for both bride and groom? If your son is an average American teenager, by the time he is fourteen he will have seen over 100,000 media examples of how to behave in sexual situations. Not that these all go straight to sex, of course, but nearly all of the media portrayals involving sexual behavior demonstrate by example that more is better and that young people should take the next step towards being sexually active.

Your son will one day find himself alone with a girl who is searching for her true identity. Culture will have convinced her that she can find meaning by giving herself sexually to your son. She will offer herself to him. What will he do? In the terror of thinking about that moment comes the recipe for training. We have spent a great deal of time talking about you and your struggle. What do you do in the moment of temptation? That is what your son needs to learn. You can teach him by example and demonstration how to approach this puzzle. How to think about what he is feeling, how to deal with what seems like irresistible temptation. Have you changed what you believe about it? I used to tell myself that the moment she is on the screen, it was all over. It was not possible to resist. So I would "accidentally" find myself in situations where she was on the screen and, sure enough, I wouldn't be able to resist. But now I don't believe that is true. I genuinely believe that if I walk into a room tomorrow and a porn movie is playing, I will simply walk back out.

Do you believe that you would simply walk back out of the room? What do you want to believe about yourself? Do you really believe that your son could wait until marriage to have sex if you didn't wait? Can you really look your son in the eye and tell him that he can wait and believe it yourself? What do you want to believe about what your son and that situation? Your influence, your honesty in sharing your struggles with him, in sharing how you have dealt with them, in pursuing his heart, in helping him see what he is really hungry for – that is the recipe. His journey has the same steps as your journey.

I feel it pressing upon me to apologize to you. I am sorry. I wish that I had a more clear formula, a set of steps for you to follow in walking with your son. Maybe a great workflow chart with penetrating questions that would lead your son to freedom in one easy conversation. Sorry. The formula consists of open-ended questions. The workflow chart is finding your son's heart. Ask him the question that will lead him to the answer instead of telling him the answer. Your life experience may have taught you that sex in high school is not the answer, but that knowledge alone will not help him when she offers herself to him. But what if he has learned from you *how to think* about what is being offered? If your conversations are full of questions like "So what were you feeling when you looked?" and "What was going on in your heart when she asked if you wanted to go further?" Men, realize that your conversation with your son after he screws up with masturbation is *perhaps the greatest teaching opportunity* you will ever have with him. DO NOT condemn. Take the opportunity to reinforce what you know is true. Your son is good. He has a new heart. One mistake does not and will not define him. *Tell him that you love him!* Ask him questions like "In that moment just before you started, what did you think you were going to feel like afterward? What were you hungry for? And how did you actually feel afterward?" Pray with him, fight for him. If you can help your son see that what is offered is never actually delivered, that it is truly false advertising, you give him the weapon to win the battle. What if you could get your son to a place where he genuinely realized that masturbation makes you feel worse afterward? What would that do for his outlook on porn? What if he really understood that porn is a poor substitute for the real hunger in his heart? What would that do for his outlook on girls? Can you imagine a boy who could look into a naked girl's eye and tell her that what he really wanted couldn't be found in her? It is possible. Your son could do that. You can help.

Your personal journey to freedom is one that you individually must take. Your Father in heaven wants to be involved. I want to be involved. You have allies. But you still have to choose to take the journey. Your son's personal journey to freedom is no different. It will be as different and as similar as your journey and my journey. Build your relationship with him. Walk with him. Start today.

And what about your girls? That is another entire book. But we have to at least mention the hard, brutal truth. Your daughter's promiscuity is a direct reflection of the validation she feels from you. We are in the middle of a cultural epidemic of fatherless young girls. Their fathers were simply unavailable to them. They never spoke the crucial words a girl needs to hear: that she is beautiful, that she is lovely, that she is worth pursuing, worth his time, that there is something about her that draws him. No, instead our culture has taught them that they can replace their dad with other men. And so they are practically throwing themselves at men in hopes of hearing the words that they were meant to hear from dad.

This may be the most brutally difficult paragraph in this entire book for some of you fathers of girls. I am truly sorry to have to write those words. But I am also the father of a young girl, albeit a five-year-old. Already I can see her looking to me to answer those core questions of her heart. And I have spoken with enough men who have sexually active daughters and broken hearts to know those words are true. Either we as fathers give them the answers or we can be sure that they will look for the answers elsewhere. It is our choice.

The good news? You can make a difference! The same lie is being told to you about your daughter as about your son. *You've messed up. You've blown it. And it's too late to do anything about it now.* Bullshit! (Sorry, I had to write that.) But that's what it is. A complete and utter lie from hell. You and you alone as her father can change her life, no matter where she is today. And just like for your son, it starts with a relationship and continues with a journey. Not of shame or guilt or pat answers, but of walking alongside her, of supporting her, of meeting her where she is and loving her and rebuilding your relationship of trust to gain the right to speak into her life. You can start that today, right now. You can do it. You have what it takes. I believe in you.

19

PRACTICAL TOOLS

Second to last chapter, men. Well done. I know the previous chapter may have been both the hardest and most inspiring so far. In writing it, my desire for freedom for both my boys and my girl has been renewed and increased. I want to end the book with the most practical, everyday, helpful tools that I know. These are tools which have dramatically helped my personal journey and the journeys of many men that I know.

The first applies to all men, single or married. In his book, *Every Man's Battle,* Stephen Arterburn offers this awesome tip. It's called the "eye bounce" and it is almost humorously simple and at the same time wonderfully freeing. We have all experienced situations where we are simply going about life, driving around, waiting at a red light, standing in line, whatever...and then she enters our view. The time of year doesn't matter, right? Winter means tight sweaters. Summer means short shorts or bikini tops. The issue is that our eyes, almost unconsciously, lock onto the beauty. In that first moment, we have not sinned, right? We're simply looking and admiring the beauty that God has created. And that lasts anywhere from a nanosecond to a full second. Then something changes and we start to go in an unhealthy direction. The simple tip? Close your eyes. Seriously. Just close them for a split second and in that second remember what you want more than a second glance. You want freedom! And in that split second, you will be amazed at how much freedom and strength you can gain. A tiny decision, a piece of your soul saved, another measure of strength earned. Just close your eyes and turn your head in another direction. And when you open them again? Freedom. Unless, as my friend, Chris, says, you are at the beach. And then you open them and close them again. Turn your head, open and close. Repeat until you find a truly great view. The pinnacle of this would be opening your eyes, seeing a gorgeous woman, thinking to yourself "Good one, God!" and shifting your viewpoint. I can tell you from experience that this tip can dramatically change the way you perceive the world. In the past, I'd see a scantily clad woman and I would take everything I could from her with my eyes. Now, I blink, look away, and often feel a sense of sorrow for her. What must her father have been like for her to dress like that? Sorrow for her is a powerful tool in choosing strength for your own freedom.

But what if the visual image of her has already moved into your mind? You shut your eyes, but your mind is off and running in a direction you don't want them to go. 2 Corinthians 10:5 tells us that we can "...take captive every thought to make it obedient to Christ." But what does that really mean? In my life, that looks like stopping myself immediately when I become aware of an inappropriate fantasy. Stopping, taking a deep breath, and praying something really simple like this:

> In the name and by the authority of Jesus Christ, I take captive this thought. I choose to not go down the path

of slavery. I choose strength. I give this thought over to Jesus Christ fully and I renounce and reject any claim being made against me this day by my enemy.

You can do this, men. I'm talking about making this an active part of your lifestyle. Car stopped at the red light, find yourself watching the gal walk through the crosswalk? Pray. Eyes lingering too long on the office coworker or secretary? Just try shutting them for three seconds and praying. I speak from personal experience when I say that this idea works wonders. God really does want to be your ally in this battle. He will come to your side and fight alongside you. But you personally have to call Him. I cannot do it on your behalf. You have to ask Him. And He will engage, I promise.

The second tip also applies to all men, single or married. Get a filter for your computer. I don't care what kind of job you have. I don't care if you have ever struggled with Internet porn. The filter is for you. It's for your wife. It's for your son, for goodness sake! And it has nothing to do with how much you trust yourself or how much you trust your son or your wife or your brother or whomever. If you have a close friend who is a former alcoholic, do you pour him a drink so that he can grow stronger by resisting the temptation to drink out of the glass sitting right in front of him? Of course not. I have a filter on my computer simply because I do not want to be surprised. It's not weakness, it is intelligent battle planning. I choose not to fight a battle that I have not prepared for. My filter helps keep me safe from those ambushes. There are a lot of filters out there, including a few free ones. The one that I have recommended to my friends is bsecure™. The website is www.bsecure.com. As of this writing, it costs $60 per year for up to three computers. I recommend this filter simply because in my experience it is ridiculously difficult and a general pain in the butt to circumvent – which, frankly, I like. I wanted something that did not break easily because, particularly early in my journey, I had several moments where I appreciated a more challenging filter. If you choose a filter similar to bsecure™, you will need to designate someone to administer the program and choose the password. You can also choose to have a report of your Internet activity emailed to that person weekly. Men, listen closely. I speak from personal experience here. DO NOT (repeat, do not) under any circumstance ask your wife to do this for you. It is not and should not be her responsibility. Find a brother you trust. Ask him to come over, install the program, and set the password. And the weekly emailed report? Let's talk about accountability right now.

Accountability is often presented by church as the best solution for a man's struggle with pornography. Unfortunately, using it *as a solution* often ends up being quite disheartening and ineffective. The reason for that ineffectiveness is the idea that only by subjecting our behavior to the review of another can we find freedom. The subtle yet tragic twist is that we are not to be trusted. Our behavior set apart from review is not to be trusted. What kind of message is that? Certainly not one that agrees with Jesus' words in Luke 4:18: "I have come...to proclaim freedom for the prisoners..." Freedom. Real freedom. Not "freedom if you don't screw up this week." Please understand, I use the concept of accountability in my life every day. With my choices, with my kids – we all do, right? Scripture is full of the idea of accountability. Romans 14:12 states that we will all be called before God to present a full accounting of our lives to Him. The issue I have with how the church uses accountability is when it is presented as being *the answer* to the problem instead of just *a tool to use* in the battle.

I have a friend, Mike, who struggles with exercising regularly. His solution has been a rather extreme form of accountability. He has written a series of checks to organizations he absolutely loathes.

A friend holds the checks and has instructions to mail them if Mike does not email his weekly exercise report. He shared with me that the current check is made out to a particularly vile (in his view) political organization that holds Hitler in high regard. So he is naturally quite incentivized to exercise regularly in order to make sure that check does not get mailed. Okay, so what does this have to do with porn and masturbation? Simply that accountability alone cannot bring you real freedom. It might help you not mess up. Great. But someone holding a hammer over your head does not mean you are living life to the fullest. Real freedom for Mike would look like his becoming the man who exercises regularly because he *wants to be that man* more than he wants to be the man who needs accountability. Most of the men I have talked with who have engaged accountability as the solution for this issue have ended up in one of two kinds of accountability groups. Group one looks like the guys who have all just decided to be okay with lying to each other. Group two looks like the guys who have all just decided to be okay with each other messing up. Accountability alone will not bring the freedom you want.

No, the beauty of accountability in this battle for freedom is as a tool. It can be an awesome weapon in this battle. An opportunity for deeper relationships here on earth. But only if we use it to build up each other. What does the subtext of accountability really speak to your heart? I mean, is there a way to interpret accountability besides – okay, you have proven yourself totally untrustworthy, so the only way you can change is to have the threat of guilt and shame hanging over your head. Sure, we couch it in nicer terms than that – helping each other, etc. But accountability is not walking with someone. It is waiting for someone to screw up so that you can nail him. And that does not build real relationships. Just like with our sons and daughters, the building block is always the relationship underneath, not the behavior we observe. The behavior is just a tool to see what is going on underneath. I am in several relationships that we might describe as accountability groups. In one, a man whom I trust and respect has asked me to be available to him if he screws up, so that he has a safe place to process what happened, to learn from it, to be encouraged, to be prayed for and fought for. And men, we need that. I have difficult seasons with pornography. A movie scene that I don't quite fully turn my head from, whatever. My heart desires a place where I can share that struggle and how I'm doing in it without being taught or instructed or shamed or told I am wrong. Accountability is about having a brotherhood of men around you who care enough about you to remind you of who you really are when you forget. That is what my band of brothers does for me. When life feels overwhelming, they remind me of who I really am.

So back to the issue at hand – what do you do about the weekly report for an Internet filter? Remember that it's about your heart. That is what is driving your behavior. Ask yourself what you want. Do you want to be held accountable by someone for what you view on the Internet? I imagine that might really be helpful for most of us. Especially if the person on the other end understands what your journey toward freedom is all about. As I shared earlier, I had a friend whom I could call anytime and find encouragement and support. I didn't need him to be the police or the guy holding the check; I needed him to be my friend. I needed a safe place to say that I was struggling and wanted help. Or that I screwed up and needed help. I do not necessarily need that anymore as I have progressed through my journey. But that does not mean I do not choose to use it from season to season depending on where I'm at in the battle. And that's the real truth about accountability: it's a tool, not the answer, in your battle for freedom.

There's another way accountability functions as a great tool as you become involved in other men's lives in this journey. If you are deeply involved in your son's life, you are going to be asking him how it's going with masturbation. And he's probably going to be asking you. Otherwise it's not real. What will your answer be when he asks you the last time you masturbated? "Yesterday." "Last week." "Two years ago, son." How powerful for him to know that it is really possible to be free. From time to time, we put on *Becoming Unbound* retreats for groups of men. During the first session of the retreat, I share my story with everyone. Part of that story is confessing the last time I masturbated. For the last five years, my report has been "The last time I masturbated was some time during the week before July 22, 2005." And you know what, men? Accountability means that I promise to always tell the truth when I tell that story. And that provides me with an amazing opportunity to make the right choice. Believe me, in times of deep temptation or struggle, I absolutely turn to that for extra motivation. What if you could tell your son the same story? That it's really truly possible to not masturbate. What might his life be like? What might yours be like? How strong do you think you would feel? Yes, accountability used correctly can be an awesome weapon in your arsenal for this battle for freedom. My friend, Eric, recently celebrated his 1,000th_ day of freedom from porn and masturbation. Does keeping that string alive add a certain amount of motivation to his journey? Absolutely! Is it the sole driving force keeping him free? Not even close. It's a tool he uses to win the battle.

The next tip does not apply to single guys, sorry. Skip to the next paragraph. But if you are married, sex with your wife is one of the most powerful tools in your freedom toolbox. First off, don't go quoting this paragraph to your wife at the end of the conversation telling her about your struggles. That probably won't go well. But physiologically and psychologically, when you stop looking at porn and masturbating, your desires don't go away. So you can choose to take all that desire and passion straight to her. There will be processing time for her and lots to work through relationally, especially if you have one-night stands, affairs, or prostitution to deal with. But just know, the best sex of your marriage is waiting for you. Your sexual relationship with your wife is an outward reflection of the inward health of your relationship. The deeper the relationship, the better the sex. In talking with older men, I have learned there is a huge lie out there that says as age sets in, sex just isn't like it used to be. And sure, there may be some truth to that in what you are physically able to do or the frequency of sex as compared with earlier in your marriage. But I have personally experienced "the best sex ever" on a pretty regular basis. And doesn't that make sense? When you hear older folks talk about their relationship with God, doesn't something inside you want the depth, the intimacy that they talk about? They know God better than we do, they have spent more time with Him, their relationship is deeper with Him, they experience a level of intimacy and satisfaction in their relationship with Him that we do not...yet. Why would marriage be any different? So pursue your wife, take all your passion and desires to her. It will spark tons of conversations and lots of opportunities to work on your communication. And it will improve your marriage. I genuinely believe that this is one of the areas where you can experience the greatest levels of freedom in this entire journey.

This next tip is for everyone, single and married, for winning the battle in the moment of temptation. First off, it is possible to win in that moment. No matter the situation. You must believe this. You always have a choice. Remember these words; they may save you untold heartbreak. *Choose* to look away. *Choose* to not take off her bra. *Choose* to walk out of the hotel room. *Choose* to close your computer. *Choose* to have your friend call ahead and block the adult movies available in your hotel room on your next business trip. *Choose strength.* You can make those choices, men! You have to really believe that! Your son can choose to walk out of the room when the high school girl offers herself to him, he really can. Do you believe that? Because if you don't, he'll be able to tell. And if you do, how you talk to him about it will shine through! You can win in the moment of temptation, sitting in front of the computer. How? By getting to this question before you commit to the sin: "What am I really hungry for? And is looking or doing this going to really satisfy that desire?" Your enemy is so good at convincing you that it will satisfy. But you have walked that road already, haven't you?!? That is why you are reading this book, right? And the answer is "No, it hasn't satisfied me, really." So do you think it will this time? Probably not. That is the key to your daily victory. Will this choice satisfy your hunger? Your life experience has almost assuredly answered the question already. The trick is to get to that pivotal mental question earlier and earlier in the temptation situation.

In my life right now, the scenario where I get to practice this concept the most lately seems to be YouTube. Somebody sent me a funny video that just ended. Invariably there is a slightly questionable video somehow linked to the one I just watched. Yesterday I was watching a video about how a compound archery bow works. Interesting and cool stuff. And then I notice over to the side there is a "sexy archery bow" video. And without even thinking, I click on it. Up comes the first slide of some gal in a halter top shooting a compound bow and I angrily click the X to close the browser window. Yes, I did it angrily, because I was pissed-off at myself. I mean, I'm writing the book on this stuff, for goodness sake, right? Yet here I am, in the moment. For the briefest window, believing that my hunger would somehow be satisfied by a stupid YouTube clip. That is the nature of our battle. Our enemy will always present opportunities, no matter how minor they seem. That video would have been rated PG. Not pornography. There was no lust on my part, no sin committed. I was angry because for that brief moment, I forgot who I was. I forgot that what I am hungry for cannot be quenched in a video. That porn and masturbation cannot satisfy the hunger of my soul.

A few years ago, Randy shared with me that he attended a counseling conference and went to a presentation by author Dr. Larry Crabb. Dr. Crabb was telling a story about being on a business trip, alone in his hotel room, flipping through the channels. He shared in the talk, "Then I came to the pay per view porn channel, and the temptation to press the 'purchase' button was tremendous, but I chose not to." And the lecture continued on to another point. After class, Randy stood in line and asked Dr. Crabb, "What made you stop? How did you resist the temptation?" Dr. Crabb replied, "I didn't deny that I wanted it, I just asked myself, *'Is there something else that I want more?'* And I thought, 'Yes, I want to be a man of God more, I want to be a strong man more than I want comfort.'"

You can choose to be a strong man, too. You can choose to keep your strength instead of giving it away. You can triumph in the moment of temptation.

The last tip is the most important. Not only can you be victorious in the moment of temptation, you can also be victorious after a moment of loss. You may lose a skirmish from time to time. It happens. We're human, we're men. Occasionally we make bad decisions. In my life right now, lost skirmishes usually look like the

YouTube clip story I mentioned above. Or an R-rated movie where I didn't close my eyes or turn my head away quickly enough. Or allowing myself to spend that extra five or ten or thirty seconds on some mental fantasy. Five years ago, I would have rejoiced at losing skirmishes like that. In the early part of my journey, lost skirmishes looked more like watching a movie that I already knew had a sex scene in it and then *accidentally forgetting* to turn my head or stopping at "just" the soft-core porn site. I also had wet dreams that turned into a skirmish. Let's take a minute and talk about wet dreams.

Physiologically, wet dreams are a normal fact of life. They function like a valve that opens when your testicles tell your brain they are storing too much old, dead sperm. Your brain tells the relevant parts to get that dead sperm out of your body. The sensation of a wet dream is similar to an orgasm because the same muscle groups are moving the sperm out. Personally, I've had around a half dozen wet dreams in my life that I was aware of. In each case, the wet dream sensations occurred along with some kind of sexual dream. I've spoken with guys who've had far more and guys who've had far fewer than I have. The important point is that you didn't do anything wrong to have one. A wet dream is 100 percent natural. If you have a wet dream, it does not mean that you have sinned. The Bible even mentions wet dreams in Deuteronomy 23:9-11 in the context of the Old Testament issue of cleanliness, not the present day issue of sin.

So why are we talking about wet dreams? Because you may have one. Because your son probably will have them. And if we don't talk about it, we give the enemy a place to go after us. Last year I was at a retreat and one of my friends, Marco, had a wet dream. He was sharing about how the enemy was really going after him hard, accusing him of all kinds of things that weren't true. As the conversation continued, I realized that he did not even know that he had had a wet dream. He had been convinced that he had somehow made himself have an orgasm because of the fantasy dream he was having. He was not aware that wet dreams even existed. Did you know? Does your son know? Can you imagine being a young man, maybe having masturbated a few times in your life, committing yourself to purity and then having a wet dream? I'm sure the enemy would be all over that, accusing, guilting, and especially shaming. We're talking about wet dreams because we need to, just like everything else in this book. Your son will need your help redeeming the moment. Your brother will too. And so will you. Because the enemy will try to convince you that losing one skirmish is the end of the battle.

In the early part of my journey, losing a skirmish felt like the end of the world. It felt like I had completely failed and could not be redeemed. We've talked a lot about your heart, about how this battle is not about perfection, about how walking with God is what will transform your life. But in the end, if you screw up, you'll have a choice to make. And I want to speak into that choice. In that moment, right after you blow it, you'll hear a voice from your enemy. *See, I told you. You are still that guy. Weak. Dirty. Different. You'll always be that guy.* Basically, you'll hear all over again the same messages you've always heard. But you'll also hear another message. *Whatever you do, don't tell a soul. You've got to keep this hidden. You are the only one who screwed up.* In the moment right after a bad decision, the enemy will want to make sure you stay alone. Because he knows that when you are isolated, he gets to rake you over the coals for as long as he wants. So how do you fight back? How do you get back on the journey toward freedom after you screw up?

First of all, and as soon as possible, get into the light. A few years ago, I heard a story about a pastor who often went to a particular restaurant for a long lunch and some study time away from the office. One day, there was a new waitress taking his order. She was the kind of person who touches others a lot. As he placed his order for lunch, her hand was resting on his forearm. She served the plate and touched his arm and shoulder. Absolutely normal. Not sinful activity. But for some reason, this pastor could not stop thinking about the feeling of her hand on his arm. And apparently this went on for several days, his reflecting on that feeling and thinking about how nice it was. And then as you can imagine, his thoughts gradually drifted toward more. He began to wonder, "Is she on at lunch again today?" "Maybe I'll take another study time this afternoon." Three days later, he said to himself, "What am I doing? This is crazy." And he called up a friend and shared the story. Immediately, the spell over him was gone. For some reason, the power of a bad thought or a message from the enemy is multiplied when we're fighting it alone. I think about all the years I spent not telling other guys about how I was doing in my battle for freedom. And how difficult it was to recover when something bad happened, which was often. And now, granted, bad things happen less often, but when they do, the power they have over me is invalidated when I share it with others. The first step to getting back on the journey to freedom is to get out of isolation, get out of the darkness, and get back into the light.

Think of losing a skirmish in battle terms. You have an enemy who is constantly looking for ways to trip you up. His end game is to separate you from God. When that happens, he wins. Period. When you are faced with temptation and make a choice to give in, the enemy loves it. He loves it because he gets to accuse you of all sorts of old lies. But his favorite part is when you stay hidden in the darkness. Then he gets to do all of those things all day long. Or all week long or month long or year long or life long. However long you stay in the darkness, he wins. In that way, shame or guilt or messages from the enemy are like a fungus. If you stay in the dark, they grow. Expose them to the light and they die. There is never a status quo. You are either winning or losing. Gaining strength or losing strength. The enemy will tell you to be quiet, to isolate, to stay out of the light. But you won't listen to him. You'll listen to the truth. And if you forget, which we all do sometimes, I've put a reminder of the truth in Appendix D of this book. Appendix D. Remember that. When all else fails and hope seems lost, please read Appendix D.

Okay, so you've gotten back into the light. You've decided to reject the lies of the enemy and remember the truth about who you really are. The next step is the three R's: repent, renounce, and reengage. In essence, you've got to get right with God, delete any messages from the enemy, and then enter the battle again. This doesn't take a long time, but it is critical that you hit each step. I'll typically spend some time with God in a prayer like this:

> Father, I come to you to get into the light. I confess (whatever you need to confess) to you. Father, forgive me. For a moment I forgot where true life is found. Thank you for forgiving my sins. I receive your cross, your shed blood, as forgiveness for my sins. I receive your resurrection and my new life. I receive your ascension as my authority and rule. I reject and renounce any agreements I have made because of this sin. If I have given any foul thought or demonic presence any permission or any influence over me because of this sin, in the name and authority of Jesus Christ I renounce that permission and influence. I command you in the name and by the authority of

Jesus Christ to be silent and leave me alone and do not return. I bind you away from me and I replace you with the truth about my identity – that I am forgiven, a child of God, and I have a new heart. I pledge my mind, soul, body, and spirit to the kingdom of God. I declare once again my freedom from sexual impurity and I choose strength from this moment forward.

20

FINAL THOUGHTS

Do you recall the scene near the end of the movie *The Matrix* where Neo is in the subway station? He turns to face his nemesis, Agent Smith. He decides to fight him instead of running away like everyone before him had done. And his friend Trinity asks their mentor, Morpheus, "Why isn't he running?" And Morpheus replies, "He's beginning to believe."

Are you beginning to believe? You are not a weak man. You are a warrior in God's image. You are not dirty or perverted. You are His new creation, with a new good heart. You have been made clean and free and empowered by the work of Jesus' death and resurrection and ascension. And you could really be free. Not a temporary freedom either. A lifetime of true freedom awaits you, my friend. Of real, genuine, life-giving freedom. It is available. This battle for your freedom has been going on for quite some time now, as you know. You have begun the journey of victory and I am so proud of you. I want to do everything in my power to help you in your journey as I continue in mine. There was a time in my life when I really believed that porn and masturbation were irresistible. But I know the truth now, that this battle is eminently winnable. You can walk away from the choice to masturbate. You can be stronger than the temptation of pornography. Read those words again, men. You are strong! You can do this! Start today! This is not an illusion, it's a real story. It's my story. And I desperately want for it to be yours.

APPENDIX A

A LETTER TO WOMEN

This is a letter written by my wife, Heather, to any woman who has just learned that her man is struggling or has struggled with pornography or other area of sexual purity.

Dear Beloved,

If you are reading this, your man has just made a confession that has broken your heart. There is a hole in your chest that wasn't there before and things feel like they may never be the same again. And it's possible this isn't the first time. I am so sorry. I don't know the exact details of your story, but I do know your pain. I am truly sorry that you have found yourself in this place. This is not how things were meant to be. You were created for something far greater, and so was your man. You were both designed to live in perfect freedom – from pain, from heartache, and from the effects of pornography. That freedom may seem far away as you read this letter. I understand. But there is hope.

When Ezra first told me that he struggled with pornography I felt like I was going to throw up. It was literally revolting to me and I could hardly even look at him – except perhaps to check my aim before I tried to kick him. We had been married less than a year and I could hardly believe this was happening. Instead of hearing my husband sharing a struggle with me, I heard all sorts of other things: *You cannot trust your husband. He is weak. He has betrayed you. This is your fault. If you were a better wife, he wouldn't have turned to porn. You will never be enough for him.* He may as well have handed me a report card on my performance as a wife with a big, old, fatty "**F**" marked across the top. How could I have failed so completely as a wife? As a woman?

Over the next eight years those lies wove their way into the daily world of our marriage. Every time Ezra would tell me that he had screwed up and looked at porn again, the lies were reinforced. He confessed three or four times after the first night. In my mind, he became weaker and weaker and less and less worthy of my respect. I felt that my failure as a wife and a woman was confirmed time and time again. Despite this, each time he confessed and asked for forgiveness, I believed it was definitely the last time. Out of blind hope and ignorance, I did my best to move on as if the problem were solved. I became "Heather the ostrich" with my head firmly entrenched in the sand. Maybe you can relate to this method of dealing with difficult situations. In truth, nothing had been solved. I had no understanding of what was really going on with Ezra. Or just how pervasive a man's struggle with pornography can be.

During the early years of our marriage, I had no idea that – depending on which study you choose to believe – 75% to 80% of married, Christian men struggle with some kind of pornography at least once per week. I thought it was an issue that only really creepy guys had to deal with. Some part of me knew that men were visually oriented, but it never occurred to me that a man's battle with pornography would last from very early in life until he's pushing up daisies. I am not sharing this to excuse your man's actions. They were wrong and almost certainly sinful and they have deeply hurt you. I am sharing this because maybe you are like I was – unaware of how big this issue really is.

Ezra finally experienced true freedom from his addiction to pornography on July 22, 2005. As he shared with me a few days later, I could clearly see that it was a different man who sat me down to share exactly what his struggle had looked like through his life and our marriage. He spoke with an honesty and a humility that I hadn't seen before. He didn't make empty promises. He told me he knew I'd need some time to process this, that he expected me to be angry and that was okay. It took incredible courage for him to do this. I'm guessing it felt a little bit like standing in front of an angry bull with a red shirt on. It took great courage for your man to tell you of his struggle with pornography as well.

I have to tell you that I was pretty pissed off after he told me. Ah, were you expecting me to say I was happy that he was finally free? But, you see, I had no idea that Ezra's struggles were as extensive as they had been. It felt like a bomb being dropped on me. I was ANGRY that he had kept such a pervasive issue from me. And, honestly, the most difficult part was that he was sharing from a place of healing – he had been freed. Freed from something I hadn't realized had been binding him so completely. But that left me in the dust. I wanted to rant at the man who had brought this garbage into our marriage, but part of me knew that *that guy* no longer existed. It was like he took my ammo away and that *really* ticked me off.

I don't want to kid you – working through my feelings and our relationship was a long process and it was no cakewalk. It was a full year before I began to trust Ezra fully again, after what felt like a sustained betrayal over the past nine years of marriage. It was closer to two years before I began to learn how to respect him. Very slowly, my picture of my husband began to change from a weak, sex-obsessed man to a strong, trustworthy man of God whose heart toward me was good. Ezra kept pursuing me during these years. Every few weeks he would ask me where I was at with our conversation, how I was feeling about his past struggles with porn, how I was feeling about him and our marriage. Even though I sometimes had trouble articulating my feelings, I loved that he kept pursuing me. He was committed to working through this thing *with* me. Part of me hated that he kept bringing it up, but he was probably just remembering my ostrich tendencies.

One of the most difficult things to work through was the lie that Ezra looking at porn was my fault. That I somehow wasn't enough to satisfy him, so he turned elsewhere. But let me tell you in no uncertain terms – IT IS NOT YOUR FAULT. I understand how it may feel like your fault, but it is not. In fact, your man's struggle has nothing to do with you, dear sister. I understand this may be hard for you to hear right now. This book is about all the reasons men struggle with porn. If you want more insight into your man, read Part II of this book, starting with Chapter Seven. It took me a while, but I finally arrived at a place where I understood that Ezra's struggles with pornography were because of his issues.

Something that also helped me during this time is that Ezra was open with me about his struggles. If he was tempted to look at porn, he shared that struggle with me. This openness took some getting used to. At first, I often felt instant terror: *Did he do it again?* But I chose to listen to Ezra and not my fear. This was crucial in my coming to trust him again. That kind of open dialogue helped rebuild the trust that had been broken during the early years of our marriage.

There is a lot more to this story than I am able to share with you here. The bigger picture involves what I learned about the heart of a woman and the heart of a man – how we were each designed and how our designs played into Ezra's and my life together. There are more resources available to you. I would recommend to you the book *Captivating* by John and Stasi Eldredge if you are interested in understanding your own heart and how God designed you. A book that will give you insight into your man is *Wild at Heart*, also by John Eldredge. And for specific understanding about men and pornography, read this book, *Becoming Unbound*.

I know you have probably just found out that your man struggles with porn and you are dealing with a lot of emotions right now. You may feel like you marriage is over, and it could be if you choose that. You could choose not to forgive him for his sins against you. But I would like to offer you a different option – an option richer and infinitely more rewarding. You can choose to press in. Fight *for* your man. Whether you realize it yet or not, you have great power to speak life into your husband. At this moment, what I'm offering you may seem difficult or even impossible, but I have found in my own marriage that being on Ezra's side has been absolutely worth it. If you choose to fight for your man and for your marriage, here are the most powerful tools I know of to keep in your handbag.

Believe in him. The number one thing you can do for your man is to believe in him. That's right. Believe in him at this moment after he has betrayed your trust. Believe in him even if he screws up. It sounds difficult, right? But one of the core things a man needs is respect. The heart of respect is your believing that he has what it takes, that he can do it. That in the clutch, he can come through. And you can't fake this. He can sniff out a fake sentiment in a heartbeat. Do you think he can remember to buy milk without a reminder? Do you think he can find his way without stopping for directions? Do you believe that he can be free from pornography? If you don't, he'll know it. He'll feel like a failure, a loser who has let you down again. But if you do believe in him he'll see it in your face and hear it in your words. Then he'll go out and conquer the world.

I actually had to ask Ezra to tell me when he felt I was being disrespectful to him – with some caveats on *how* to tell me in a way I could receive, of course! I was honestly not aware of that my actions were disrespectful a lot of the time. Perhaps you aren't either. Often it did not make any sense to me what he saw as disrespectful – my girl brain just doesn't work the same way. But, it doesn't have to. The only thing that needs to make sense is your decision to believe in your man.

Don't try to manage him. You may be tempted to manage your man by trying to control his situation. Perhaps you secretly check up on his computer activity or install a filter behind his back or call him to "innocently" check-in a bit more often. This is absolutely the worst possible thing you can do. Let me ask you a question. How do you feel when someone is trying to manage you? Now, perhaps you are nicer than I am, but I start kicking and screaming (literally and figuratively) pretty quickly. Magnify that by about four million, and you have the average man's reaction. Being managed goes against a man's design. His wild heart is meant to lead. Any attempt to control or manage my man *always* backfires in a hurry.

Don't withhold sex. Another thing you may be tempted to do is to withhold yourself sexually from your husband. Believe me, I tried it and it backfired. Keeping sex as a tool to punish your husband is a sin according to 1 Corinthians 7:5 (NIV). It is also not helpful in any way and will only serve to worsen your marriage. Men receive love two ways – through respect and sex. Keeping sex from your husband will not punish him or teach him not to look at porn, it will only make him feel deeply rejected and unloved. Do not hear me say that you need to go have sex with your husband tonight. There may be some serious consequences of his poor decisions. It's possible he's been unfaithful in a way that needs medical intervention, testing, or health care before you are intimate with him again. Again, I'm not talking (necessarily) about tonight. I'm talking about the next part of your journey toward a deeper relationship and a better marriage.

Learn about what he's dealing with. If you want to know what it's like to be a man who struggles with pornography, if you want to understand your man better, learn about what he's dealing with. Read this book. Part I is the story of Ezra's personal struggle, told in as frank a way as possible. Part II details Ezra's journey toward freedom. These chapters will shine a light on what your man has been dealing with and the freedom that is available to him (and you).

Walk with him in it. Be his partner in his struggle with pornography. That looks like listening to him when he wants to talk about how he's feeling and how things are going for him. In the beginning I had a difficult time listening to Ezra without getting upset and hearing unintended blame in his words. This was a journey for me, but today we can talk openly about how things are going for him. And that's crucial for him because it means that I understand that the journey has ups and downs. Our men may screw up, they may have some difficult habits to break, but with our help the battle will be easier.

Your man's struggle with pornography is a difficult and painful thing. But you have already taken the first step in the journey to fight for him. You chose to read this letter instead of throwing the book at him. Good work. After five years of fighting for Ezra, my marriage is better than it ever has been. Ezra and I are far from perfect, but we are definitely in this together. You will have to take your own journey and no doubt it will look different than mine. One thing I know is that if you choose to fight for your man and seek God together, you will find your way to a stronger marriage and a greater love for your God and your man.

You can do this. I believe in you. My heart is for you and I will be fighting alongside you through prayer.

Heather Snyder, August 2010

Appendix B
The Daily Prayer

This prayer is reprinted with permission from Ransomed Heart Ministries. I can tell you from experience that praying a prayer like this will dramatically impact your day for the better. It's not a formula, you don't have to pray it word for word. But it is the compilation of hundreds of verses throughout Scripture that tell us who we are as believers and what blessings and authority have been given to us. I recommend that it become part of your daily routine, slowly praying through each paragraph, making it personal, adding your thoughts and desires and heart into the mix.

My dear Lord Jesus I come to you now to be restored in you, to be renewed in you, to receive your love and your life, and all the grace and mercy I so desperately need this day. I honor you as my Sovereign, and I surrender every aspect of my life totally and completely to you. I give you my spirit, soul, and body, my heart, mind, and will. I cover myself with your blood — my spirit, soul, and body, my heart, mind and will. I ask your Holy Spirit to restore me in you, renew me in you, and to lead me in this time of prayer.

In all that I now pray, I stand in total agreement with your Spirit, and with my intercessors and allies, by your Spirit alone.

[Now, if you are a husband, you'll want to include your wife in this time of prayer. If you are a parent, you'll want to include your children. If this doesn't apply to you, jump to the paragraph after this one.]

In all that I now pray, I include (my wife and/or children, by name). Acting as their head, I bring them under your authority and covering, as I come under your authority and covering. I cover (wife and/or children, by name) with your blood – their spirit, soul, and body, their heart, mind and will. I ask your Spirit to restore them in you, renew them in you, and apply to them all that I now pray on their behalf, acting as their head.

Dear God, holy and victorious Trinity, you alone are worthy of all my worship, my heart's devotion, all my praise, all my trust and all the glory of my life. I love you, I worship you, I trust you. I give myself over to you in my heart's search for life. You alone are Life, and you have become my life. I renounce all other gods, all idols, and I give you the place in my heart and in my life that you truly deserve. I confess here and now that this is all about you, God, and not about me. You are the Hero of this story, and I belong to you. Forgive me for my every sin. Search me and know me and reveal to me where you are working in my life, and grant to me the grace of your healing and deliverance, and a deep and true repentance.

Heavenly Father, thank you for loving me and choosing me before you made the world. You are my true Father – my Creator, my Redeemer, my Sustainer, and the true end of all things, including my life. I love you, I trust you, I worship you. I give myself over to you to be one with you in all things, as Jesus is one with you. Thank you for proving your love by sending Jesus. I receive him and all his life and all his work, which you ordained for me. Thank you for including me in Christ, for forgiving me my sins, for granting me his righteousness, for making me complete in him. Thank you for making me alive with Christ, raising me with him, seating me with him at your right hand, establishing me in his authority, and anointing me with your Holy Spirit, your love, and your favor. I receive it all with thanks and give it total claim to my life – my spirit, soul, and body, my heart, mind, and will. I bring the life and the work of Jesus over (wife and/or children, by name) and over my home, my household, my vehicles, my finances, all my kingdom and domain.

Jesus, thank you for coming to ransom me with your own life. I love you, I worship you, I trust you. I give myself over to you, to be one with you in all things. And I receive all the work and all of the triumph of your cross, death, blood, and sacrifice for me, through which I am atoned for, I am ransomed and transferred to your kingdom, my sin nature is removed, my heart is circumcised unto God, and every claim made against me is disarmed this day. I now take my place in your cross and death, through which I have died with you to sin, to my flesh, to the world, and to the evil one. I take up the cross and crucify my flesh with all its pride, arrogance, unbelief, and idolatry (and anything else you are currently struggling with). I put off the old man. I ask you to apply to me the fullness of your cross, death, blood and sacrifice. I receive it with thanks and give it total claim to my spirit, soul and body, my heart, mind and will.

Jesus, I also sincerely receive you as my life, my holiness, and my strength, and I receive all the work and triumph of your resurrection, through which you have conquered sin and death and judgment.

Death has no mastery over you, nor does any foul thing. And I have been raised with you to a new life, to live your life – dead to sin and alive to God. I now take my place in your resurrection and in your life, through which I am saved by your life. I reign in life through your life. I receive your life – your humility, love, and forgiveness, your integrity in all things, your wisdom, discernment, and cunning, your strength, your joy, your union with the Father. Apply to me the fullness of your resurrection. I receive it with thanks and give it total claim to my spirit, soul, and body, my heart, mind, and will.

Jesus, I also sincerely receive you as my authority, rule, and dominion, my everlasting victory against Satan and his kingdom, and my ability to bring your Kingdom at all times and in every way. I receive all the work and triumph of your ascension, through which you have judged Satan and cast him down, and you have disarmed his kingdom. All authority in heaven and on earth has been given to you, Jesus. All authority in heaven and on earth has been given to you, and you are worthy to receive all glory and honor, power and dominion, now and forevermore. And I have been given fullness in you, in your authority. I now take my place in your ascension, and in your throne, through which I have been raised with you to the right hand of the Father and established in your authority. I now bring the kingdom of God, and the authority, rule, and dominion of Jesus Christ over my life today, over my home, my household, my vehicles and finances, over all my kingdom and domain. I now bring the authority, rule and dominion of the Lord Jesus Christ, and the fullness of the work of Christ, against Satan, against his kingdom, against every foul and unclean spirit come against me. (At this point you might want to name the spirits that you know have been attacking you). I bring the full work of

Jesus Christ against every foul power and black art, against every human being and their warfare. I bind it all from me in the authority of the Lord Jesus Christ and in his Name.

Holy Spirit, thank you for coming. I love you, I worship you, I trust you. I sincerely receive you and all the work and victory in Pentecost, through which you have come, you have clothed me with power from on high, sealed me in Christ. You have become my union with the Father and the Son, become the Spirit of truth in me, the life of God in me, my Counselor, Comforter, Strength, and Guide. I honor you as my Sovereign, and I yield every dimension of my spirit, soul, and body, my heart, mind, and will to you and you alone, to be filled with you, to walk in step with you in all things. Fill me afresh. Restore my union with the Father and the Son. Lead me in all truth, anoint me for all of my life and walk and calling, and lead me deeper into Jesus today. I receive you with thanks, and I give you total claim to my life.

Heavenly Father, thank you for granting to me every spiritual blessing in the heavenlies in Christ Jesus. I claim the riches in Christ Jesus over my life today, my home, my kingdom, and my domain. I bring the blood of Christ over my spirit, soul, and body, my heart, mind, and will. I put on the full armor of God – the belt of truth, breastplate of righteousness, shoes of the gospel, helmet of salvation. I take up the shield of faith and sword of the Spirit, and I choose to wield these weapons at all times in the power of God. I choose to pray at all times in the Spirit.

Thank you for your angels. I summon them in the authority of Jesus Christ and command them to destroy the kingdom of darkness throughout my kingdom and domain, destroy all that is raised against me, and to establish your Kingdom throughout my kingdom and domain. I ask you to send forth your Spirit to raise up prayer and intercession for me this day. I now call forth the kingdom of the Lord Jesus Christ throughout my home, my family, my kingdom, and my domain, in the authority of the Lord Jesus Christ, with all glory and honor and thanks to him.

APPENDIX C
STUDY GUIDE

The purpose of this section is to help you build allies and go deeper into this journey of freedom. I envision you and a friend meeting for coffee, working through these questions, genuinely engaging each other and sharing your stories with each other. I would suggest that the most rewarding time will be found simply sharing your stories and thoughts on each question. Avoid the temptation to try to fix your friend's situation or answer his questions. It's a journey that we are all on, just share! My experience has been that this type of brotherhood is incredibly powerful in affecting your journey for the better. Each chapter of the book has three or four questions designed to encourage you to go deeper into the material and deeper into your own story and life experiences. Take some time with these. If you don't own a journal, go buy one. Allow yourself at least one journal page per chapter to leave room for note-taking or jotting down thoughts as you ponder the questions.

Chapter One: Early Years

- When was the first time you saw pornography?

- When was the first time you masturbated?

- What kind of home did you grow up in? Christian? Non-Christian?

- What was the general view on pornography in your home?

Chapter Two: Dark Years

- What were your adolescent years like in the battle with pornography and masturbation?

- What were your twenties, thirties, forties, fifties, sixties like in the battle with pornography and masturbation?

Chapter Three: Bottom of the Barrel

- What was the lowest point in your life in your battle with porn and masturbation?

- How far did you take your bad desires?

- What have you lost because of your struggle? Jobs? Relationships?

Chapter Four: The Island

- Share a few stories about seasons of victory in your battle with porn and masturbation.

- What did you believe about yourself during those seasons of victory?

- What did you believe about yourself when those seasons of victory ended?

Chapter Five: The Journey Begins

- Have you heard God speak to you about anything in your life?

- What would you love to hear Him say about you?

- What are you afraid He might say?

Chapter Six: Becoming Unbound

Instead of questions for this chapter, I will suggest a group activity. Find a day when you can all dedicate at least a few hours together. Go somewhere peaceful where you can escape the noise. Turn off everything electronic. Pray together, separate for an hour, take a walk, sit in the sun, whatever. Ask God what He wants to talk about. Listen. Come back together and talk about what you heard or didn't hear. Share your hearts about what you want to hear, your frustrations, whatever is happening in your heart. Pray together, then spend another hour listening individually. Come back together and talk. Repeat as you desire.

Chapter Seven: The Playing Field

- Was your church experience similar to this?

- Do you believe that porn is a sin? What about masturbation?

- What misconceptions have you had about these definitions throughout your life?

Chapter Eight: The Battle

- What is your reaction to the idea that you could be a man after God's own heart? Do you honestly believe that could be true about you?

- Share your perspective on the concept of the war, battle, and skirmish.

- What do you think about the idea that the battle is for your deep heart?

Chapter Nine: D-Day

- Share your personal D-Day story if you already have one.

- If you have not yet had a D-Day, pray together right now or plan a time to make your commitment to independence.

Chapter Ten: Your Enemy

- Share your perspective on spiritual warfare prior to reading this book.

- What kinds of spiritual warfare have you experienced in your life?

- Do you really believe that your struggle is not with flesh and blood, but with principalities and powers? (Eph. 6 NIV) How is that belief changing your behavior?

Chapter Eleven: Understanding Your Heart

- How do you feel about the idea that your desires are fundamentally good?

- Do you agree that your desires are good?

- How angry are you at God for not answering your prayer to take the desires away? Do you understand now why He did not?

Chapter Twelve: Burning Your Card

- Are there situations in your life where you believe that you do have the right to look at pornography or masturbate? What are those situations?

- What steps must you take to change your mind that you have that right?

- Have you burned your card? If not, find a time to do so together.

Chapter Thirteen: Hunger

- Describe the circumstances when you feel the draw of pornography or masturbation most strongly. Work-related? Wife-related?

- In those moments, what do you feel? The desire to be strong? The desire to feel taken care of, loved? The desire to escape?

- What are you really hungry for in those tempting moments? If God spoke to you at that exact moment, what could He say that would truly fill you up?

Chapter Fourteen: Identity

- What messages have you heard about your identity through-out your life? Weak, dirty, different? What else?

- How do you think God sees you as a man? What words do you think He would use to describe you?

- Find another chunk of time to spend together as a group pursuing God. Use the exercise at the end of Chapter Fourteen. Find a peaceful place, find some space. Pray together, then spend some time pursuing God, asking Him what He thinks of you. Come back together and share. Repeat.

Chapter Fifteen: Allies

- Share how you have experienced community or brotherhood in your life.

- Do you have any allies in your life right now in this battle for freedom?

- What would you love for this group of men to become? Share your dreams with each other.

- Share any roadblocks in your life to a more full alliance with God. How has that been for you in the past? What do you want it to look like in the future?

- Share how the exercise at the end of Chapter Fifteen went.

Chapter Sixteen: Clearing the Cache

- What caches do you have that need clearing?

- Do you have any that need backup? Coordinate that time right now.

- Do you need any group prayer for any specific mental or spiritual caches? Share how praying through those is bringing freedom. If it isn't, try praying together as a group.

Chapter Seventeen: Telling Your Wife

- What do you need to confess to your wife?

- How do you plan to do that? Setting? Timing? Explanation?

- What areas do you want prayer for as you prepare to tell her?

Chapter Eighteen: Walking With Your Son

- What do you want for your son, regardless of how old he is?

- Share the state of your current relationship with him. Are you at a place where you can talk deeply about things like porn and masturbation? What work might need to happen in the relationship first?

- How do you intend to pursue your relationship with him? What (if anything) is going to be different in how you relate with him to help you earn the right to speak into his life at a deeper level? What would "Lego time" look like for him right now?

Chapter Nineteen: Practical Tools

- Share your perspectives on some of the tools mentioned in this chapter.

- Do you have a filter on all the computers in your house? Why not?

- Share a couple ways that you would like help from the other men in your group in winning this battle for freedom.

Chapter Twenty: Final Thoughts

- Are you beginning to believe that you are not *that guy* anymore? Share how your belief about that has changed since Chapter One.

- What is the next step for you in your personal journey toward freedom?

- What is the next step for this group together?

Please allow me to suggest an answer for this last question, assuming that each of you (whether there are two of you or four or five) wishes to go deeper together. A fantastic next step would be to go through the book *Wild at Heart* and the accompanying *Field Manual*. You'll need to purchase both the book and the manual. I have gone through this with groups of men on several occasions. Taking this seriously will require at least six months of meeting weekly but can easily go for a year if everyone in your group is invested and sharing deeply. And it will be well worth your time!

Appendix D
D-Day Renewed

I'm torn between heartbreak and hope if you are reading this. Heartbreak because you've blown it. I understand, believe me, I've messed up, as you know. But I am still sorry that you did. Hope, though, because screwing up is not the end of the story. My good friend, Joe, attended the very first Unbound study in May 2006. He made a D-Day commitment and burned his card. In August, I knew something was wrong. He was avoiding me, changing the subject whenever Unbound came up. Later on, he would share with me how he felt ashamed and could not find the courage to tell me that he had lost a skirmish. He felt like he had failed and all hope had been lost. But a couple months later, at another retreat, he had another D-Day. That was almost four years ago, and he has been walking in freedom and choosing strength ever since.

All that to say – you are not alone. Do not believe the lies of your enemy. He would love for you to believe all sorts of things and come to all kinds of conclusions about yourself because of a poor decision. Remember that they are lies. He is still selling the same lies about being weak, dirty, and different that he's been selling your whole life. And they still are not the truest thing about you. And so, once again, you have a choice.

You can choose to believe the lies of your enemy. He would love that. He wants you to feel weak; that makes him happy. Or you can choose to remember that losing one skirmish does not mean that you've lost the battle. He'll try to convince you of that, of course. But it's just not true. Yes, you need to confess your sin or sins. Yes, there may be consequences because of your behavior. But, no, one choice does not define who you are unless you allow it to.

So choose strength, again, my friend. I believe in you. I know that you can do it. I know your heart is truly good, that you want freedom and life to the full. So choose freedom right now!

> Father, I come to you to get into the light. I confess (whatever you need to confess) to you. Father, forgive me. For a moment I forgot where true life is found. Thank you for forgiving my sins. I receive your cross, your shed blood, as forgiveness for my sins. I receive your resurrection and my new life. I receive your ascension as my authority and rule. I reject and renounce any agreements I have made because of this sin.

> If I have given any foul thought or demonic presence any permission or any influence over me because of this sin, in the name and authority of Jesus Christ I renounce that permission and influence. I command you in the name and by the authority of Jesus Christ to be silent and leave me alone and do not return. I bind you away from me and I replace you with the truth about my

identity – that I am forgiven, a child of God, and I have a new heart. I pledge my mind, soul, body, and spirit to the kingdom of God. I declare once again my freedom from sexual impurity and I choose strength from this moment forward.

Good. Now re-engage, brother! If you have a group of friends, tell them what happened. Trust me, they will thank you for doing so! If you don't, drop us a line at www.unboundministries.com. Make a connection somewhere. Don't stay in the dark about this. Get into the light and stay there!

And re-read this book. Pray the Daily Prayer in Appendix B tomorrow morning. Take action. I believe in you. You can do this! You can choose strength!